Mary & the Saints

Marian Consecration

Mary & the Saints

Marian Consecration

by
Ruthie Greenhalgh

www.maryandthesaints.com

Consecration Start Dates & Marian Feast Days

Start Date	Consecration Date	
November 29	January 1	Solemnity of Mary, Mother of God
December 6	January 8	Our Lady of Prompt Succor
December 31	February 2	Purification of the Virgin Mary
January 9	February 11	Our Lady of Lourdes
February 20	March 25	The Annunciation
March 24	April 26	Our Lady of Good Counsel
March 26	April 28	Feast day of Saint Louis-Marie de Montfort
March 29	May 1	Queen of Heaven
April 10	May 13	Our Lady of Fatima
April 28	May 31	Feast of the Visitation
May 7	June 9	Mary, Mother of Grace
May 25	June 27	Our Lady of Perpetual Help
June 13	July 16	Our Lady of Mount Carmel
June 30	August 2	Our Lady of the Angels
July 2	August 5	Our Lady of the Snows
July 11	August 13	Our Lady, Refuge of Sinners
July 13	August 15	The Assumption of Mary into heaven
July 20	August 22	The Queenship of Mary
August 6	September 8	Birth of the Virgin Mary
August 10	September 12	The Most Holy Name of Mary
August 13	September 15	Our Lady of Sorrows
August 22	September 24	Our Lady of Mercy
September 4	October 7	Our Lady of the Rosary
September 13	October 16	The Purity of the Blessed Virgin Mary
October 19	November 21	Presentation of the Blessed Virgin Mary
November 5	December 8	Immaculate Conception
November 9	December 12	Our Lady of Guadalupe

Office of the Archbishop

Imprimatur

In accordance with the provisions of canon 830 §3, having received a favorable opinion from Michael Podrebarac, Censor Deputatus, and by my authority as Archbishop, I am pleased to grant an *Imprimatur* for the book entitled *Mary & the Saints Marian Consecration*, authored by Ruthie Greenhalgh.

If the *imprimatur* is to be acknowledged, the following declaration is required to be included:

> The *nihil obstat* and *imprimatur* are declarations that the work is considered to be free from doctrinal or moral error. It is not implied that those who have granted the same agree with the contents, opinions, or statements expressed therein.

Given at the Chancery of the Archdiocese of Kansas City in Kansas on the 15th day of April in the Year of Our Lord two thousand twenty-one.

Most Reverend Joseph F. Naumann
Archbishop of Kansas City in Kansas

Reverend John Riley
Chancellor

This book is dedicated to:
Ellie Greenhalgh, my original intended audience.
My family for their encouragement and support
in everything I do, including the writing of this book.
My fiancé, Nick Dellasega, my sweet path to Heaven.
My mama Mary for continuing to lead me deeper into the
Sacred Heart of Jesus, the greatest love of my life.

Special thanks to:
My proofreaders Kate Greenhalgh, Fr. Mark Ostrowski,
and my editor Jeffrey Cole.

Table of Contents

Introduction

I have always had an interest in people's stories. When I was in high school, I directed my energy towards celebrities' lives and eventually collected four large boxes of *People* magazines and kept them in my closet—that is until my mother found out and made me get rid of them because, apparently, they were a fire hazard.

I've heard that after you encounter Jesus your interests and talents don't change, but become purified and manifest themselves in a new way—a way that will glorify God and work for the salvation of souls.

I grew up in a very faithful Catholic family that ended each evening by praying the Rosary together, but it was not until I was twenty-seven years old and in the middle of my first Marian Consecration, *33 Days to Morning Glory* by Fr. Michael Gaitley, that I really encountered Jesus in a life-changing way. It wasn't through any huge event, but in a dark and empty Church after a daily noon Mass during Lent in 2012. In just one moment, I encountered the most tender and powerful love, and I knew that for the rest of my life I wanted to do whatever I could to help others experience that too. I have no doubt that it was Mary who, through the consecration, brought me right to the Sacred Heart of Jesus, initiating that encounter.

After that, I still had an interest in the lives of others, but I now turned more to the lives of the saints. Their lives were exciting and unique, and, in learning about them, I was able to learn new ways to grow in my relationship with Jesus.

Then, in the summer of 2020, the idea for this Marian Consecration was born. In prayer, I felt that Mary was inviting me to write about the saints and others who have gifted the Church with their Marian devotions and teachings. However, it seemed like too big of a task. But, towards the end of the summer, my sister and I decided to do a Marian Consecration for Mary's birthday on September 8. This would be my sister's first time consecrating herself to Jesus through Mary, and she wanted something that would help her learn about the saints too. I knew this was my opportunity. So, every day between August 6 and September 8, we learned about a new person and their Marian devotion.

As St. Louis de Montfort tells us, Mary is the surest, easiest, shortest, and most perfect means by which to go to Jesus.[1]   She brings us to Jesus. I believe this because I have experienced it in my own life and watched how she has obtained blessings for all those who ask for her intercession, even blessing generations.

My hope is that through this consecration you are able to encounter Jesus in a new way through the powerful intercession of His mother and the men and women in these pages who want to accompany you as you walk the path they have already taken.

Ruthie Greenhalgh
March 4, 2021

---

[1] See St. Louis de Montfort, *True Devotion to Mary*, 55.

Day 1

Venerable Fulton Sheen
(1895–1979)

Fulton Sheen was born Peter John Sheen in El Paso, Illinois, on May 8, 1895. One of four boys from a devout Catholic family, he got the nickname Fulton (his mother's maiden name), and it stuck. When his family moved to Peoria, Illinois, he served as an altar boy at St. Mary's Cathedral and, as a teenager, discovered his vocation to be a priest.

Throughout his life, he was known for many things: a brilliant and engaging speaker who taught the Catholic Faith in a fresh and clever way that his audience would understand, a teacher of philosophy at Catholic University, a national radio host of *The Catholic Hour*, an enormously successful television host who was awarded two Emmys for the Most Outstanding Television Personality (even beating Lucille Ball), an author of over sixty books, and Bishop of Rochester. But, perhaps, what he would most like to be known for are his devotion to Mary and his daily Holy Hour.

Mary was the great love of Sheen's life, and it was his love for her that led him to a deeper devotion and love for Jesus, especially Jesus in the Eucharist. We will see this was the case for many of the great Marian saints and actually the point of a Marian Consecration—to have Mary lead us to have a deeper and more faithful love for Jesus.

While he wrote a lot about Mary and the importance of her intercession, including the book *The World's First Love*, we are going to focus on one of his insights. Sheen explains that God has two pictures of us: the picture of who he created us to be and the picture of who we truly are. For us, there is a gap between the two, and the main reason for this gap is sin. The more we sin, the more we are pulled away from the person God created us to be. But, as Sheen said, there is one person in whom there is no gap, and that is Mary. Mary is exactly who God created her to be.[2]

---

[2] See Fulton J. Sheen, *The World's First Love* (Garden City, NY: Garden City Publishing Company, 1953), 4–5.

Mary wants to intercede for us and fill the gap between who we are and who God created us to be. And, by filling it, Mary helps us turn away from sin and towards God and the mission He created us for. We can also ask Mary to fill the gaps in our lives and hearts in other ways as well. We can ask her to fill the gap between the love we can give and the love that others need, and the love that we need and the love that others can give. Any time we feel that we are in need or coming up short, whether it be in love, in time, in performance, or in prayer, we can simply ask Mary to fill the gap, and she will.

Fulton Sheen died on December 9, 1979, the feast of another great Marian saint, Juan Diego. Sheen's cause for canonization was opened in 2002, and he is currently a venerable, the second of the four steps in the Church's canonization process—servant of God, venerable, blessed, and saint. Episodes of his show *Life is Worth Living* can be found on YouTube.

Mary, please fill the gap.

Venerable Fulton Sheen, pray for us.

Day 2

Saint Juan Diego
(1474–1548)

Saint Juan Diego, whom we mentioned yesterday (Fulton Sheen died on his feast day), was a native of Mexico, who lived at the same time as the Protestant Reformation. While the Church was facing the loss of millions to Protestantism in Europe, Spanish missionaries were having their own difficulties in proclaiming the Gospel to the indigenous people of Mexico.

This lack of missionary success was partly because the missionaries weren't trusted by the indigenous people due to their language barrier, and then, what the people did understand, they didn't want to hear about. They were already weighed down by their own cruel gods who they believed demanded human sacrifice, particularly the sacrifice of their children. So, after more than twenty years of effort, the missionaries had little to show for it. But two of the few people who did convert were a poor man named Juan Diego and his wife, Maria Lucia.

One day, in December 1531, two years after the death of his wife, the fifty-seven-year-old Juan Diego was on his way to church when he was visited by a woman on Tepeyac Hill. She revealed herself as the Virgin Mary and asked that a chapel be built there in her honor to better serve the people who asked for her intercession. When Juan Diego presented this request to the bishop, he was almost immediately dismissed. However, upon further thought, the bishop decided to ask Juan for a sign from Mary to confirm that the request came from her. When Juan told Mary about the bishop's request, she agreed and directed Juan to a field of roses, instructing him to pick them and place them in his tilma where she rearranged them and sent him back to the bishop.

Now, Mary is a lover of details. The roses were flowers that were originally from a region near the Holy Land but were popular in the part of Spain that the bishop was from. They did not grow in Mexico and did not grow anywhere in the dead of winter. That was Mary's detail for the bishop.

When Juan went back to the bishop, he opened his tilma to show the roses. However, when the roses fell, a beautiful image of Our Lady appeared on Juan Diego's tilma. This image, now known as the image of Our Lady of Guadalupe, proved to be full of small but important details that would lead over nine million indigenous people to convert to Catholicism in less than ten years. Why? Because Mary spoke the language of the people who communicated mainly in hieroglyphics, telling them that there was one true God and that He was a God who loved them. In fact, God's tremendous love for them was proven a few days later. An indigenous man was brought back from the dead when his body was placed in the presence of the tilma. It was a shock for the people who were used to their gods demanding death. Yet here was a God, who, through His mother, gave life.

Here are a few of the details of the image of Our Lady of Guadalupe that converted millions of indigenous people in Mexico to the Catholic Faith:

- The way that her hair is parted down the middle indicates that she is a virgin, her black belt indicates that she is pregnant, and the four-petaled flower over her womb was their symbol for the divine. Through the image, Mary was telling them that she is a virgin pregnant with God.

- The color of her skin was the same as theirs, showing them that she was one of them.

- She is in the process of doing their victory dance—with her hands together, she is jumping on one foot (notice that one of her knees is bent)—indicating that she is victorious over even their most powerful gods, including their sun god, whom she is standing in front of, and their god of darkness (symbolized by the moon), whom she is standing on top of.

Over the past five hundred years, scientists have studied the tilma, and many have converted after what they have discovered. Some of their more recent discoveries include:

- In 1979, doctors magnified Mary's eyes to 2,500X. They found people, including Juan Diego and the bishop, reflected in her eyes exactly in the manner that the human eye would reflect an image.

- The stars on her tilma mirror the constellations in the night sky on December 12, 1531—the day the tilma was revealed. Amazingly, the arrangement of the stars is from God's perspective looking upon the universe rather than us looking at the stars from Earth.

This tilma is just one example of our Mother who is detailed, powerful, and always interceding for us.

Mary, take care of the details.

Saint Juan Diego, pray for us.

Saint Dominic
(1170–1221)

When talking about St. Dominic, it is nearly impossible not to talk about the name of Mary, as pious tradition assigns Dominic the honor of receiving the Rosary directly from her hands. Dominic was born in Spain, the youngest of three boys, and was the answer to the prayer of his mother, Blessed Jane of Aza, who is herself one step away from canonization as a saint. After her two older sons were grown and had left to become priests, Dominic's mother asked God for another son. Shortly after her prayer, she had a dream in which she saw a dog leaping forth from her womb carrying a torch in his mouth. She understood this to mean that her prayer was heard and her child would go forth and set the earth on fire for God. This image of a black and white dog with a flaming torch in its mouth is one of the symbols of the Dominican Order, and, early on, the Dominicans received the moniker *Domini canes*, which is literally translated as "Hounds of the Lord."

When he was twenty-five, Dominic became a priest and preached for several years in Spain with great success before going to France to combat the heresy known as Albigensianism. The Albigensians thought that the spirit was good but that matter and all material things were evil. Because of this, they believed that people were actually spirits trapped in evil bodies. Following this line of thinking, they also denied the Incarnation of Christ and His Real Presence in the Eucharist. This proved to be a devastating heresy as thousands of people broke away from the Church to follow it.

But all was not lost. Hearing the desperate prayers of Dominic, God allowed Mary to intervene. According to pious tradition, Our Lady appeared to Dominic and presented him with the Rosary—the weapon that would end Albigensianism. Soon after, Dominic and a group of priests who joined his mission, later called the Order of Preachers (or Dominicans), set out to re-convert the Albigensians and spread the devotion of the Rosary. Due to their preaching, over 100,000 people came back to the Catholic Faith, and, eventually, the Albigensian heresy ended. Through the

Rosary and the intercession of Mary, Dominic and his Order of Preachers performed miracles, cured the sick, and even raised people from the dead, always by invoking the name of Mary. In the years that followed, devotion to the Rosary spread throughout the entire Church.

Mary gave fifteen promises to those who are faithful to the Rosary, including the dispelling of heresy. The power of the Rosary is so great that we can't even comprehend all of its spiritual benefits. Lucia, one of the children to whom Mary appeared in Fatima, said: "There is no problem, I tell you, no matter how difficult it is, that we cannot solve by the prayer of the Holy Rosary."[3]

Fun fact: Michelangelo's painting of the Last Judgment in the Sistine Chapel has two souls being saved from Hell by the Rosary.

Mary, give us the grace to be faithful to the Rosary.

Saint Dominic, pray for us.

---

[3] Kathleen Hattrup. "There's No Problem, No Matter How Difficult, That the Rosary Can't Solve." Aleteia (January 14, 2020): aleteia.org/2020/01/14/theres-no-problem-no-matter-how-difficult-that-the-rosary-cant-solve/.

Day 4

Blessed Bartolo Longo
(1841–1926)

Bartolo Longo was born in Brindisi, Italy, in 1841, to a wealthy and devoutly Catholic family that prayed the Rosary together every night. At the age of ten, when one of his parents passed away, he began to drift away from God. When it was time for Bartolo to go to college, Italy's leaders had begun an anti-Catholic movement in an attempt to overthrow the pope and destroy the Catholic Church so as to "unite" Italy. This movement became increasingly popular among young adults, especially those in college. Some of Bartolo's professors at the University of Naples were ex-priests who openly spoke out against the Church. Having slowly drifted for so long, this proved to be the deciding factor in Bartolo's own departure from the Faith. But Bartolo was a smart and zealous young man, and simply leaving the Church was not enough. Fueled by the hatred spewed by his professors, he began attending satanic rituals and, eventually, was "ordained" a satanic priest, promising his soul to the devil. He spent his time speaking out against the Church and convincing others to join him.

The more he practiced the satanic rituals, however, the more Bartolo descended into deep depression and darkness. He began to experience extreme paranoia, confusion, and nervousness. Always on edge that he would suffer another vision of Hell, something that happened to him periodically, his anxiety continually escalated until he was on the verge of a mental breakdown.

Bartolo's family back home was devastated that he had abandoned the Faith and continued to pray the Rosary for his conversion. One night in his sleep, Bartolo heard the words, *Return to God! Return to God!*[4] He had reached his breaking point, so he sought out a professor he knew was a practicing Catholic. The professor, in turn, introduced him to a Dominican

---

[4] Angelo Stagnaro. "The Satanist on the path to sainthood." Catholic Herald (July 13, 2011): catholicherald.co.uk/the-satanist-on-the-path-to-sainthood/.

priest who listened to his story and helped him return to the Catholic Church, hearing his confession and absolving him of his sins.

Bartolo was a new man—he had life again! But even though his sins were forgiven, the memories of the decisions he had made against God would still sometimes haunt him and tempt him to believe that he had gone too far to be saved and truly forgiven. When expressing these doubts to the Dominican priest, he was told to pray and to promote the Rosary because Mary promises that those who do so will be saved. In time, he developed a great love for Mary and gratitude that she would intercede for his salvation even after all he had done against the Church. With a newfound energy and determination, Bartolo began praying and promoting the Rosary to all who would listen. Later, he would become a Lay Dominican and take the name Brother Rosary.

After moving to Pompeii, Italy, Bartolo was shocked at how little the people knew about their Catholic Faith. He helped fund and restore a church, rededicating it to Our Lady of the Rosary. Bringing the people back to Jesus through the intercession of Mary and her Rosary, Bartolo helped to breathe life back into the town. When Bartolo was given an old image of Our Lady of the Rosary with St. Dominic and St. Catherine of Siena at her feet, he immediately had the image restored and hung in the church. Soon, stories of countless miracles started coming from those who visited the church, making it a place of prayerful pilgrimage for visitors. It is now known as the Basilica of Our Lady of the Rosary of Pompeii.

For over fifty years, Bartolo promoted the Rosary and its saving effects. As a friend of Pope Leo XIII, he encouraged the pope to continue writing encyclicals on the power of the Rosary. Bartolo Longo is known as the Apostle of the Rosary and is currently a blessed in the Church, the third step in the canonization process.

Mary, give us confidence in the promises of the Rosary.

Blessed Bartolo Longo, pray for us.

Day 5

Pope Leo XIII
(1810–1903)

Pope Leo XIII was born Vincenzo Pecci in 1810, in Rome, Italy, the sixth of seven boys. He has the honor of being the oldest pope (he died at the age of ninety-three), having reigned for twenty-five years, the third longest reign in Church history. Overall, Pope Leo XIII had a tremendous impact on the Church and the world at large. He encouraged schools, especially universities and seminaries, to teach the writings of St. Thomas Aquinas, a practice still common today, and authorized the building of the Catholic University of America. He also played a key role in the lives of countless saints who were alive in his day by personally meeting with them and encouraging their vocations. Some of these saints include Thérèse the Little Flower, Katharine Drexel, John Henry Newman, Frances Xavier Cabrini, and Bl. Bartolo Longo.

His great love for Mary began as a young adult when he read St. Louis de Montfort's *True Devotion to Mary*—not long after its discovery after having been hidden for over one hundred years!—and consecrated himself to Mary using de Montfort's form. Along with promoting de Montfort's writings, Pope Leo XIII also promoted St. Bernard of Clairvaux's Marian writings, and he was the first pope to refer to Mary as Mediatrix, a teaching of St. Bernard. Pope Leo also tirelessly promoted the Rosary and its power. Out of his eighty-eight encyclicals—a number unheard of at the time!—eleven were about the Rosary. (To put things in perspective, John Paul II wrote fourteen encyclicals throughout the course of his twenty-six-year papacy, and Pope Benedict XVI wrote three.) Because of this, Leo is known as the "Rosary Pope." He said in one of his encyclicals, "The rosary is the most excellent form of prayer and the most efficacious means of attaining eternal life. It is the remedy for all our evils, the root of all our blessings. There is no more excellent way of praying."[5]

---

[5] Shaun McAfee, *I'm Catholic, Now What?* (Huntington, IN: Our Sunday Visitor, 2019), chpt. 36.

There is one story in particular about Pope Leo XIII that happened on October 13, 1884, exactly thirty-three years before the Fatima miracle of the sun. That morning, while the pope was celebrating his private Mass, he overheard a conversation between God and Satan. In it, Satan said that if he was given enough time and power, he could destroy the Catholic Church. In order to refute him, God permitted Satan to unleash his power over a span of one hundred years, which is believed to have been the twentieth century. Hearing this conversation shook the pope greatly, and, immediately after Mass, he wrote the prayer to St. Michael the Archangel—the leader of the heavenly army who cast Satan out of Heaven when he rebelled against God. The pope instructed that this prayer should be prayed after every Low Mass.

St. Michael is our great defender from Satan, but there is a great Marian connection here too. Mary, the crusher of Satan, is the Queen of the heavenly army. As St. Louis de Montfort says in *True Devotion to Mary*, "Even St. Michael, though prince of all the heavenly court, is the most eager of all the angels to honor her and lead others to honor her. At all times he awaits the privilege of going at her word to the aid of one of her servants."[6] So we must call on Mary, and she will send the great heavenly armies to defend us in our battles.

Mary, send St. Michael and the heavenly army to defend us in battle.

Pope Leo XIII, pray for us.

---

[6] St. Louis de Montfort, *True Devotion to Mary*, 8.

Day 6

Saint Gemma Galgani
(1878–1903)

Gemma Galgani was born in Lucca, Italy, in 1878, the fifth of eight children. Unfortunately, her early childhood was met with terrible heartbreak, losing her mother and three of her siblings to tuberculosis when she was still a little girl. At sixteen, she herself suffered from spinal meningitis but was cured thanks to the miraculous intercession of two saints whom she loved: St. Margaret Mary Alacoque and St. Gabriel of the Sorrowful Mother. Gemma's father died when she was eighteen, leaving her to care for her surviving siblings. During this time, she decided to become a housekeeper, yet turned down two different marriage proposals because she dreamed of one day becoming a nun in the Passionist Order.

By this time, Gemma had developed a great love for Jesus in the Eucharist and for Mary, specifically under the title Co-Redemptrix, the same title Pope Leo XIII loved to use. Gemma had a strong desire to save sinners through her prayers and would spend hours praying each day in her room, talking with Jesus and begging him to save souls. Gemma was also a mystic, having frequent visits from Jesus, Mary, and her guardian angel. Particularly, every Thursday night, the three of them would come to her, and Jesus would allow her to feel the sufferings that He felt the night before His Passion and Death. She considered it a great privilege to share in the sufferings of Jesus whom she loved so much. But still the pain would be too much, and Mary would stand behind her, wrap Gemma under her mantle, and lift her up so that she wouldn't collapse on the ground in pain.

One night, Gemma was in her room, begging the Lord to give the grace of repentance to a young man in town. This man was in deep sin, although from the outside it looked as if he was living a perfect Christian life. For hours, Gemma begged with fervor for this man to be saved. She implored Jesus, reminding Him of all that He suffered in His Passion specifically for that young man. But, no matter how much she prayed, she felt like she was being met with Jesus the Just Judge instead of Jesus the

Merciful Savior. Finally, after hours of exhaustive prayer, Gemma was about to give up, when it occurred to her to go to Mary. She told Jesus that she would go to Mary and let her ask Him. Jesus replied that He could never refuse His mother anything. Gemma found out later that it was within the hour of her request to Mary that the priest received a knock at his door, and the very young man for whom Gemma had been praying threw himself at the priest's feet, sobbing and begging for him to hear his confession. Mary had obtained the grace from Jesus for him to repent and change his ways, and, from that moment on, he zealously served the Kingdom.

Gemma died at the age of twenty-five from tuberculosis, the same disease that had taken so many of her family members. She was canonized in 1940, and, even though she was not able to become a Passionist nun due to her early death, she is known as the Daughter of the Passion.

Mary, please ask Jesus for the grace of repentance for us, for we know that He can refuse you nothing.

Saint Gemma Galgani, pray for us.

Day 7

Saint Teresa of Ávila
(1515–1582)

Saint Teresa of Ávila was born in Ávila, Spain, in 1515, two years before the beginning of the Protestant Reformation, and sixteen years before Our Lady of Guadalupe appeared to Juan Diego. A very outgoing, lively, and fun girl, she was one of nine children born into a wealthy family. Her outer spunk was balanced by an inner awareness and love for God and natural affection towards Mary. As a young adult, Teresa decided to join the local Carmelite Order, a convent that was known for its lack of discipline and the "go-to" spot to get the town gossip. For the first twenty years that Teresa was in the convent, her relationship with God was like a roller coaster—she would sometimes enter deeply into prayer, but then the things of the world would pull her away and cause her to be distracted.

When she was forty, Teresa finally decided to take her vocation as a Carmelite nun seriously. She sought out the company of those who were striving to live a holy life, and, at the advice of her confessor, worked to blot out even the smallest venial sins in her life, as these were the things that were keeping her from fully entering into her relationship with God. She started avoiding the gossip and instead took Mary as her confidant in a renewed way. She began praying the Rosary with great devotion, a habit she acquired from her own mother. Over the next twenty years of her life, Teresa followed the example of Mary and made herself available to God and the work He wanted to do in and through her.

Teresa soon became a master of prayer and was later named a Doctor of the Church. Known for her deep and mystical prayer life, she taught her fellow sisters the different stages of the spiritual life, always speaking of the deep riches that came from meditating on the Rosary. She taught from her own experiences and spoke about lofty subjects in plain language, stressing the importance of developing a "heart relationship" with Jesus and Mary based on love to further advance in the spiritual life. While the intellectual

17

side of the Faith can better explain what is experienced in the heart, it cannot replace it. She explained that it is in the heart that we encounter Jesus and our lives are changed.

Teresa was especially devoted to what is called the Brigittine Rosary (from St. Bridget of Sweden), which has six decades instead of five. The first five decades are prayed like a normal Rosary and the sixth decade is dedicated to events in the life of Mary. When she set out to reform her own and other Spanish Carmelite convents, bringing them back to the focus on prayer and recollection, she instituted the Brigittine Rosary as part of their habit.

Teresa's impact on the Carmelites, and the Church at large, is evident in some of her fellow saints that came after her. Sts. Thérèse the Little Flower and Teresa Benedicta of the Cross (Edith Stein) were both named after her. Teresa's deep theological insights mixed with her simplicity is the perfect image of what devotion to the Rosary can look like.

Fun fact: When Mary appeared to Bernadette at Lourdes, she appeared with the six-decade Brigittine Rosary.

Mary, help us to develop a "heart relationship" with you and your Son.

Saint Teresa of Ávila, pray for us.

Saint Edith Stein
(1891–1942)

Edith Stein, also known as St. Teresa Benedicta of the Cross, was born in 1891, the youngest of eleven children in a Jewish family living in Poland. Even though she admired her family's religious faith, Edith became an atheist in her teenage years. After serving as a nurse for the Red Cross in World War I, she became an academic by profession. Studying philosophy, she developed a particular interest in phenomenology, the study of structures of consciousness as experienced from the first-person point of view[7], which, at the time, was in its beginning stages. By contributing significant insights to these fields, Edith is considered one of the most brilliant philosophers of the twentieth century.

By the time she was thirty, Edith, following her search for the truth, and after reading the works of St. Teresa of Ávila, was drawn to the Catholic Faith. Following her Baptism, she left the university world and, after delaying her decision to become a Carmelite nun out of respect for her Jewish mother, spent the next ten years teaching at an all-girls Dominican school. During those years, Edith continued to contribute to the world of philosophy. Looking through a Catholic lens, Edith wrote extensively on the role of women and the "feminine genius." She spoke specifically of four feminine traits, which we will examine, especially in regard to how they were perfectly embodied by Mary:

- **Receptivity:** While women have a physical space for another in their womb, they also have a space for another in their very being. Women are created to receive others, but everyone (both male and female) is first and foremost created to receive God and His gifts. Mary at the Annunciation (see Lk 1:26–38) is our example for perfect receptivity,

---

[7] David Woodruff Smith. "Phenomenology." Stanford Encyclopedia of Philosophy, Stanford University (December 16, 2013): plato.stanford.edu/entries/pheno-menology/.

and Edith echoed St. Augustine when she taught that Mary's *fiat* was the strongest act of free will and that each Christian is called to imitate her total yes to God.

- **Generosity:** Generosity naturally follows receptivity. In order to give to others and to be generous with our time and love, we must first receive from God. Mary at the Visitation (see Lk 1:39–56) shows us this when, after the Annunciation, she goes "in haste" to her cousin Elizabeth, ready to bring her the God she had just received.

- **Sensitivity:** The awareness that women have towards the needs of those around them, and the tendency to be more emotionally invested in others' lives. We can look to Mary at the Wedding of Cana (see Jn 2: 1–11) as the prime example of this trait. Mary was aware of the needs of the people even before the people themselves were!

- **Maternity:** "To be a mother" (physical or spiritual), as defined by Edith, "is to nourish and protect true humanity and bring it to development."[8] This is exemplified by Mary at the foot of the Cross (see Jn 19: 25–27), when she received John (and, in turn, the whole Church) as her son. Edith refers to Mary several times in her writings as the Mother of the Church, who nourishes, protects, and intercedes for us, her children, so we can become the people that God created us to be.

Throughout this time, between becoming Catholic and joining the Carmelite Order, Edith was led to a deeper love for Jesus, especially in the sacraments. In fact, after she was able to reflect on her own life, she concluded that we will never become the people we are created to be outside of the sacraments, something that she took very seriously. Along with her commitment to daily Communion, she also spent the first hour of her day with Jesus in Eucharistic Adoration, recognizing the importance of this time and the benefit it would have on everyone she would encounter throughout the day.

Finally, in 1933, after eleven years at the Dominican school, Edith was able to become a Carmelite nun, an order whose patron is Mary under the title of Our Lady of Mount Carmel. Taking the name Teresa Benedicta of the Cross, in honor of St. Teresa of Ávila, she spent her time in the

---

8 Fr. Michael Rennier. "With her particular brand of feminism, Stein is a voice for modern times." Aleteia (April 23, 2017): aleteia.org/2017/04/23/7-edith-stein-quotes-that-all-women-need-to-hear-today/.

convent praying, writing, and teaching until August 1942, when the Nazis arrested her for the "crime" of being a Jewish Catholic convert.

Edith Stein was killed on August 9, 1942, in the gas chambers of Auschwitz Birkenau, along with her sister Rosa, who had become a Third Order Carmelite and lived at the convent as well. Despite all of her professional achievements, Edith's lifelong search for truth that eventually led her to the Truth was the greatest achievement of her life.

Mary, lead us to the Truth.

Saint Edith Stein, pray for us.

Day 9

Saints Louis and Zélie Martin
(1823–1894) (1831-1877)

Saints Louis and Zélie Martin have the unique honor of being the first married couple to be canonized as saints together. Both were born in France in the early nineteenth century to devout Catholic families, and both attempted to join religious orders as young adults, but each was rejected. Accepting God's will in their lives, each continued their strong faith life as they set out for the working world. Louis became a clockmaker, and Zélie a lace maker. Their paths crossed on a bridge in the small town of Alençon, France, when Louis was thirty-four and Zélie was twenty-seven. While neither of them spoke to each other as they passed, Zélie heard a voice say, *This is the one I've prepared for you.*[9] Not long after that, they officially met and dated for three months before getting married at midnight on July 12, 1858, in the Basilica of Notre Dame in Alençon.

The Martins entered their marriage with a great love for Mary and a deep devotion to Jesus in the Eucharist. Every day of their marriage, they walked to the 5:30 am Mass at the Church next door, and Louis went to Adoration every afternoon. When setting up their home, they took their three-foot statue of Mary as the Immaculate Conception and set it up in a prominent place, resolving to end their evenings by kneeling in front of it in prayer. All of their petitions and prayers passed through the hands of Mary. Whenever anyone they knew traveled to Paris, Zélie always requested that a candle be lit for them at the statue of Mary in Our Lady of Victories Church. When her younger brother moved to Paris to attend pharmacy school, she requested he light a candle and say a Hail Mary at that statue every day for his own conversion. It ended up working, and he became a devout Catholic with a special devotion to Our Lady of Victories.

---

[9] Céline Martin, *The Mother of the Little Flower*. Zélie Martin, 1831–1877 (Rockford, IL: TAN Books, 2005), 3.

The Martins prayed that, through Mary's intercession, God would give them children that they could raise up for Him and were, in time, blessed with nine: seven girls and two boys. They gave each child, both girls and boys, the first name Marie and consecrated each of them to Mary in front of their family statue. While only five of their children, all girls, lived past childhood, they continued their habit of ending every night kneeling in prayer in front of Mary, and the children all kissed her hands before heading off to bed. In the Marian month of May, the Martins decorated the statue with flowers from their garden. The children later said that in the eyes of their mother, Zélie, nothing was too beautiful or extravagant for the Virgin Mary.

The Martins also turned to Mary in times of heartache and pain. When Zélie was diagnosed with breast cancer, when her youngest was still a toddler, she traveled with her three oldest daughters to Lourdes to ask Mary to intercede for her complete healing. Even though she did not receive the physical healing she prayed for, she was given the spiritual strength to submit to God's will. Zélie ended up dying when her youngest was only four and a half years old.

Following the death of his wife, Louis moved his family from Alençon to Lisieux, France, and continued to instill in his children a love for Mary. All five of the Martin girls became nuns, and all entered Marian Orders: four of them entering the Carmelites, and one of them entering the Visitation Order. Louis and Zélie's hidden and seemingly ordinary life gained recognition when their youngest daughter, Thérèse, better known as St. Thérèse the Little Flower, was canonized a saint.

Mary, help our families turn to you as our intercessor.

Saints Louis and Zélie Martin, pray for us.

Day 10

Saint Thérèse the Little Flower
(1873–1897)

Saint and Doctor of the Church, Marie Françoise-Thérèse, better known as Saint Thérèse the Little Flower, was born on January 2, 1873, and immediately became the delight of her family. She was always known as "little" Thérèse to her family because, two years before she was born, they lost their infant baby whom they had also called Thérèse. Her birth was cause for great celebration and thanksgiving after the family suffered the loss of four children in less than four years.

Thérèse's love for Mary began early thanks to the Marian devotion practiced in her family. In addition, through her experiences of Mary's motherly and personal love, Thérèse developed her own special love for her. Seeing how much Mary was honored in the Martin home, Thérèse could easily recognize Mary as Queen. Seeing the maternal heart of Mary, Thérèse realized that while Mary was Queen, she was mother first. Once, after her mother, Zélie, died, Thérèse went to Mary, fully abandoning herself into her arms with the same love and trust as she had done with own mother, knowing she would be safe in the arms of her heavenly mother.

When Thérèse was nine years old, she became very sick, prompting her family to turn to Mary, as they always did, to pray for Thérèse's healing. One evening, weak and scared, Thérèse turned to the family statue of Mary and uttered her own prayer to Mary. Suddenly, she saw Mary come alive and, with such motherly love, smile at her. In that instant, Thérèse was cured and, from then on, they referred to the statue as "Our Lady of the Smile." After she was healed, Thérèse accompanied her father to Adoration as often as she could, deepening her devotion to Jesus in the Eucharist. On the day of her First Communion, wanting to receive Jesus with as much love as she could, she consecrated herself to Mary, so that, when she received Jesus, He would feel like He was resting in the heart of His mother.

By the time Thérèse was fourteen, her soul had been set on fire with love for God, and she was determined to bring as many souls as possible to Him. Knowing her prayers alone could not save sinners, she relied fully on Mary to help her achieve this goal. The first person she decided to offer her prayers and sacrifices for was a convicted murderer, Henri Pranzini, who was on death row. After months of Thérèse's prayers and offerings, the man showed no sign of remorse until the day of his execution when Thérèse begged Mary to intercede. As he walked to the guillotine, Henri suddenly shouted for a Catholic priest to give him absolution for his sins, and, when he received it, he kissed the crucifix repeatedly just before his death. This answered prayer increased Thérèse's desire to pray and sacrifice more for sinners and console the heart of Jesus with Mary.

After being given special permission to enter the Carmelites at age fifteen by the Carmelite superiors, she joined two of her sisters who were already in the Carmelite Order. They would later be joined by another sister, Celine. Continuing to pray and sacrifice for sinners, Thérèse found in Mary the perfect model. Recognizing that no one did the will of the good God more perfectly than Mary, Thérèse followed her example and tried to love God in the hidden and humble ways of her daily life, trusting that Mary would help her. Thérèse lived as a Carmelite for nine years before dying at age twenty-four from tuberculosis. She kept Mary as her constant companion throughout her illness and took comfort in knowing that when her time came, her heavenly mother would come, take her into her arms, and bring her to Heaven.

Mary, when our time comes, take us into your arms and bring us to Heaven.

Saint Thérèse the Little Flower, pray for us.

Day 11

Saint Teresa of Calcutta
(1910–1997)

Agnes Gonxhe Bojaxhiu was born in Albania in 1910, the youngest of three children in a loving and faithful family. Despite the turmoil that her country was experiencing at the time, her family nurtured in her a deep devotion and love for Jesus and Mary. When she was still a girl she decided that she wanted to serve God by joining a missionary religious order, and, at age eighteen, she left her family and joined the Sisters of Loreto, an Irish Order of missionaries serving in India. Once a sister, she took the name Teresa, after St. Thérèse the Little Flower, co-patron of missionaries.

After living her vocation as a Sister of Loreto for over twenty years, teaching and serving as headmistress for an all-girls Catholic school in Calcutta, India, Mother Teresa experienced, in 1946, what she described as a "call within a call" while on the train to her annual retreat. She felt that God was asking her to leave her religious order and serve the poor of Calcutta to allow them to experience the love that God had for them. After several years, her request to do this was granted and, in 1950, she left the safe walls of the Sisters of Loreto to begin the Missionaries of Charity.

Mother Teresa had a great love for Mary throughout her life. The Sisters of Loreto is a Marian Order, named in honor of the house of Loreto where the Annunciation occurred. When Mother Teresa received the "call within a call," she said that it was Mary who was by her side, explaining to her what Jesus was asking. In the years after founding the Missionaries of Charity, a time that spanned almost fifty years, Mother Teresa suffered silently from what is known as the "Dark Night of the Soul" in which she no longer felt God's presence. Throughout this intense suffering, she relied heavily on Mary.

Mother Teresa had two specific prayers to Mary that she would repeat throughout her days. The first one was "Mary, my mother, please be a mother to me now."[10]   After having grown up with such an affectionate earthly mother, Mother Teresa felt her absence severely when she left home to join the Sisters of Loreto. In times of great homesickness throughout her life, she would ask Mary to allow her to feel her motherly love.

The second prayer to Mary that was always on her lips was, "Mary, lend me your heart and keep me in your most pure heart."[11]   This prayer stemmed from her overwhelming love for Jesus and the desire to love Him perfectly, even though she could not feel His love in return. Mary's heart is perfect, so, in asking her to lend it, Mother Teresa was asking to love Jesus perfectly. She was also asking Mary to keep her in her heart, so she might always remain close to Jesus. This short prayer summarizes the essence of Marian Consecration. We give ourselves to Mary in order to be led closer to Jesus, and we ask for her heart in order to love Jesus perfectly.

Mary, our mother, please lend us your heart so that we may love Jesus perfectly and remain close to Him always.

Saint Teresa of Calcutta, pray for us.

---

[10] Cerith Gardiner. "Try Mother Teresa's 5-second prayer to Mary for when you need support." Aleteia (December 13, 2020,): aleteia.org/2020/12/13/try-mother-teresas-5-second-prayer-to-mary-for-when-you-need-support/.

[11] Fr. Michael Gaitley, *33 Days to Morning Glory* (Stockbridge, MA: Marian Press, 2011), 113.

Day 12

Saint Francis of Assisi

(1181–1226)

Usually we associate St. Francis of Assisi with poverty or his love of animals (Francis would preach to the animals when people wouldn't listen to him!), but we don't normally associate him with his love for Mary. However, as St. Bonaventure tells us, St. Francis "loved with an unspeakable affection the Mother of the Lord."[12]

St. Francis was born in Assisi, Italy in 1181, to a wealthy Italian man and his French wife. He was given the name Giovanni, but, as a boy, his dad called him Francesco, meaning "French boy," a nod to his mother's homeland, and the name stayed with him. Francis, who was very well-liked by the people of Assisi, spent his time socializing with his many friends and dreaming of the day when he could become a knight in Assisi's army.

He thought his dreams had finally come true when he went off to do battle for Assisi against a rival army. Unfortunately, he was captured during the battle and left in a dungeon for almost a year. During this cold and quiet imprisonment, he got his first real taste of prayer, but, shortly after his release, he continued on with his old lifestyle. After several years of restlessness in which he experienced short spurts of prayer or meditation, Francis again went off to battle. However, one night, as he lay on the ground of the army campsite, he had a dream in which he heard God ask him, *Francis, who is it better to serve, the Master or the Servant?*

Francis answered, *The Master.*

The voice then said, *Go back to Assisi and all this will be yours.*[13] So, he did.

Like his contemporary and friend St. Dominic, St. Francis founded a new religious order that reinvigorated a Church in ruins. Some years

---

[12] St. Bonaventure, *Legenda Maior*, IX, 3.
[13] "A Brief Account of the Life of St. Francis." Capuchin Franciscans Australia: capuchin.org.au/about-us/st-francis-of-assisi/.

later, when Francis and a few of his followers were in Rome trying to get official permission from the pope to begin their new religious order, he had a dream in which he saw God about to unleash severe punishments on the world in response to humanity turning away from Him. Mary, however, came and begged God to show His mercy and forgiveness. She then presented Him with two men who would labor for the conversion of the world and bring countless people back to the Faith. Francis recognized himself as one of the men, but it wasn't until the next day, when he was introduced to St. Dominic, that he recognized the other man in the dream. Dominic also recognized Francis because he had had the same dream as well. This began a lifelong friendship for the two, laboring together in the fields of the Lord, although physically far apart.

As Francis's love and devotion to Mary continued to grow stronger, he would often meditate on the Wedding Feast at Cana, specifically Mary's instructions to "do whatever He tells you" (Jn 2: 5). Francis wanted to live by these words so wholeheartedly that when Jesus spoke to him from the crucifix and implored him to "rebuild my Church,"[14] Francis immediately began repairing the church he was praying in. It wasn't until later that he understood that Jesus was asking him to rebuild the Church at large.

Years after the Franciscans were founded and were laboring hard for the Kingdom, Francis had another dream. Jesus was showing him two ladders reaching towards Heaven. He watched as his friars tried to climb the ladder that was red and very steep, indicating a hard and treacherous climb ahead of them. After climbing a few rungs, they would suddenly fall back. Jesus then showed Francis the other ladder leading to Heaven, white and much less steep, at whose summit appeared the Blessed Virgin, indicating an easier way to reach Heaven to be with Him. Jesus said to Francis: "Advise your sons to go by the ladder of My Mother."[15] So, he did.

Mary, help us to "do whatever He tells us" (Jn 2: 5).

Saint Francis of Assisi, pray for us.

---

[14] "Francis Rebuild My Church." Church of St. Francis of Assisi: stfrancisnyc.org/francis-rebuild-my-church/.

[15] "Blessed Virgin Mary: Mary, Queen of the Friars Minor Capuchin." Capuchin Franciscans: capuchins.org/blessed-virgin-mary/.

Saint Clare of Assisi
(1194–1253)

Saint Clare, who was also from Assisi, had a deep friendship with St. Francis. Born into a family of nobles and knights in 1194, she was the oldest of three girls and destined for an easy life—that is until she encountered the preaching of a local man named Francis. Clare would sneak away and listen to Francis preach in the streets, totally captivated by his message. Her heart burned to follow him, but two major roadblocks threatened to stop her. For one, her father would never give permission for her to leave home and renounce her inheritance and future. Additionally, Francis had no women in his new religious order. But still she continued to listen to him preach and even confided in Francis about her desire to leave everything and follow in his footsteps.

Finally, one night when Clare was eighteen, she felt God's call to join Francis so strongly that she snuck out of her house and found Francis praying in his chapel. As she arrived at the door, she could hear him praying the ancient prayer to the Holy Spirit, *Veni Creator Spiritus*. She approached him and told him she was there to stay. Neither knew how to move forward, but both knew the Holy Spirit would lead.

Even though her father was furious at her for leaving everything, he could not convince her to return home. In fact, shortly after Clare left, her sister Agnes, only eighteen months younger and her constant companion, joined her as well. Slowly, more women followed Clare's lead, and eventually she founded the Order of Poor Ladies (renamed the Poor Clares after her death), the first women's branch of the Franciscan Order. Clare became the first woman ever to write a Rule (a document that governs and guides the members of a religious order).

Through it all, Mary was Clare's model and inspiration. Clare looked to her when saying yes to something that had never been done before. Clare also felt a deep kinship with Mary because of her role in the life of Francis. Clare wanted to be for Francis what Mary is for Jesus, a follower who furthers his mission.

Clare is another saint whose love for Mary goes hand in hand with her love for the Eucharist. Her faith and trust in the Eucharist were so strong that one day, when an army of Saracen soldiers were descending upon Assisi in attack, Clare took the Blessed Sacrament outside and faced it towards the army, unafraid and with total trust that Jesus would protect her order and the city. As the Saracens approached, they suddenly became terrified and fled the area leaving the nuns and the city in peace.

Clare's yes to an untrod path changed the lives of countless people after her, including the members of her own family. Along with Agnes, who is also a saint, her mother, Ortolana, and her youngest sister, Beatrice, followed her into the order and both have been beatified, which is the third step in the canonization process.

Mary, help us to say yes to what God is calling us to, even if it hasn't yet been done.

Saint Clare of Assisi, pray for us.

Day 14
Saint Catherine Labouré
(1806–1876)

Saint Catherine Labouré, who was born in 1806, played an important role in the Church's declaration of the Dogma of the Immaculate Conception of Mary, which stated and reaffirmed the Church's belief that Mary was conceived without Original Sin. She also played a pivotal role in the events that furthered the development of devotion to the Immaculate Heart of Mary over the next one hundred years.

Catherine Labouré was the ninth of eleven children born to a farming family in France. When she was only nine years old, Catherine's mother died, and she and her sister were sent to live with their aunt. However, before she left home, Catherine went over to a statue of Mary and entrusted herself to her care, saying, "You are my mother now."[16]

It was to this little girl that Mary appeared fifteen years later, in 1830, in a tiny convent chapel in Paris, France. The twenty-four-year-old Catherine was now in her first year of novitiate as a Daughter of Charity. When Mary appeared, she seemed to be standing on the world and crushing a serpent under her feet with light streaming from jewels on her fingers. She told Catherine to have a medal made with that image on it, along with the words, "O Mary, conceived without sin, pray for us who have recourse to thee." The back of the medal was to have the images of the Sacred and Immaculate Hearts and a cross with a large M surrounded by twelve stars.

Catherine brought the request to her spiritual director and, two years later, the medals were made. Due to the words on the front, the medal became known as the Medal of the Immaculate Conception. But, as the medals spread, stories of miracles began pouring in. People from all over the world were experiencing the power of Mary's intercession through this medal. In fact, there were so many miracles that the medal soon became known as the Miraculous Medal.

---

[16] "Roses for Mary." An Teaghlach Naof: anteaghlachnaofa.ie/roses-for-mary-feb17.html.

One thing Catherine noticed when Mary appeared was that while light was coming from some of her fingers, it wasn't streaming from all of them. Catherine asked why this was and Mary said that the light represented the graces she obtains for those who ask. The fingers with no light streaming from them represented the graces that were available but not given because no one asked for them.

After this apparition, Catherine lived the next forty-seven years of her life in virtual anonymity. Only her spiritual director knew that she was the one Mary appeared to with the request of this medal. It wasn't until the year that she died that she revealed this secret to her Mother Superior. Catherine's body, which is displayed in the chapel of the Miraculous Medal apparition, is incorrupt, meaning it has not suffered decay.

Mary, please obtain for us all of God's graces.

Saint Catherine Labouré, pray for us.

Day 15

Marie-Alphonse Ratisbonne
(1814–1884)

Marie-Alphonse Ratisbonne was a Jewish French atheist, who converted to Catholicism as an adult. Although he has not been declared a saint, his conversion came about through a miracle of a miraculous medal.

Alphonse, as he was known before his conversion, was born in 1814, the eleventh of thirteen children. When he was a young boy, his older brother, Theodore, converted from Judaism to Catholicism and became a priest. This experience not only devastated Alphonse but caused a lot of heartache in his family, which led Alphonse to despise the Catholic Church. This attitude toward the Catholic Church continued into his adulthood when he became a very successful and wealthy banker.

In 1842, after getting engaged, he decided to travel before his wedding. While originally wanting to visit the island of Malta, Alphonse boarded the wrong boat and ended up in Rome. He decided to stay there a few days and arranged to meet up with a friend. Through this friend, Alphonse met a man who had recently converted to Catholicism. After learning this fact, Alphonse set out to dissuade him from his faith, and, after several heated arguments, they decided to make a bet. The friend challenged Alphonse to wear a miraculous medal around his neck and pray the *Memorare* prayer once in the morning and once at night for ten days. If nothing happened, then Alphonse could be satisfied with his view of the "ridiculous nature" of Catholicism.

Towards the end of the ten days, Alphonse decided to accompany the man to a Church, Sant' Andrea delle Fratte (St. Andrew of the Woods), where they were preparing for a funeral Mass. Staying true to his end of the bargain, Alphonse had the miraculous medal around his neck when he entered. As the man was busy with funeral preparations, Alphonse decided to walk around the Church. When he reached a side altar dedicated to St. Michael the Archangel, the entire Church suddenly went dark, except one spot where a bright light shone. Alphonse saw the most beautiful woman he had ever seen. She didn't say anything, but he had a sense that he was

35

supposed to kneel out of reverence. Immediately he saw all the sins of his life, and, in that instant, was infused with all the knowledge of the Catholic Faith, including the understanding that Catholicism was the fulfillment of Judaism. The whole apparition lasted only a few minutes. When his friend came to find him, Alphonse knelt weeping on the floor, kissing over and over again the miraculous medal he wore around his neck.

Not long after, he was baptized and decided to add "Marie" to his name because of his great love for Mary. He became a Catholic priest and, together with his brother Theodore, set out to evangelize in the Holy Land. He remained there until he died and is now buried at the site of the Visitation. To this day, this is the only approved Marian apparition in Rome.

Seventy-five years after the conversion of Marie-Alphonse Ratisbonne, Maximilian Kolbe celebrated his first Mass as a priest in Sant' Andrea delle Fratte at the side altar where Mary had appeared. This story of conversion confirmed Maximillian Kolbe's belief in the power of the miraculous medal and solidified his decision to found the Militia Immaculata.

Memorare

Remember, O most gracious Virgin Mary, that never
was it known that anyone who fled to thy protection,
implored thy help, or sought thine intercession,
was left unaided.

Inspired by this confidence, I fly unto thee, O Virgin of virgins,
my Mother. To thee do I come, before thee I stand, sinful
and sorrowful.

O Mother of the Word Incarnate, despise not my petitions,
but in thy mercy hear and answer me. Amen.

Mary, never leave us unaided.

Marie-Alphonse Ratisbonne, pray for us.

Day 16

Saint Bernadette Soubirous
(1844–1879)

As a young teenage girl, Bernadette Soubirous was witness to one of the most wide-reaching apparitions of the Blessed Virgin Mary. Bernadette was born in 1844, in Lourdes, a small town tucked away in the Pyrenees mountains of southwest France. She was the oldest of nine children in a family that was extremely poor, and, while they were Catholic, their faith could be described as lukewarm at best. By the time she was fourteen, Bernadette hardly knew the Hail Mary and definitely did not know what had been unfolding in the Church for the last twenty-eight years.

In 1854, twenty-four years after Mary appeared to Catherine Labouré asking her to have a medal made with the words, "Oh Mary conceived without sin, pray for us who have recourse to thee," the pope promulgated the third Marian dogma, the Immaculate Conception of Mary. A dogma is a revealed teaching of Christ that is proclaimed by the magisterium for the belief of the faithful. In this case, the Dogma of the Immaculate Conception proclaims the truth that, from the moment of her conception, Mary was preserved from all stain of Original Sin.

Four years later, on February 11, 1858, while walking with her sister and a friend, Bernadette suddenly saw a lady dressed in white. Although she was with the other two girls, Bernadette was the only one who could see her. This would be the first of eighteen times that Mary would appear to Bernadette, though our focus today will be on just two of these times: the first being Mary's response when Bernadette, at the request of her parish priest, asked Our Lady who she was. Mary replied, "I am the Immaculate Conception."[17] Bernadette did not know what that meant but repeated it to herself over and over until she reached the priest and told him what Our Lady had said. The priest was shocked because, while he knew of the recently

---

[17] Colette Lienhard. "I am the Immaculate Conception." The Arlington Catholic Herald (November 23, 2020): catholicherald.com/Faith/_I_am_the_Immaculate_Conception_/.

proclaimed dogma, he also knew there was no way Bernadette could have known.

In another apparition, two weeks after the first visit, Mary instructed Bernadette to "drink of the water of the spring, to wash in it and to eat the herb that grew there"[18] as an act of penance. These apparitions were happening by the side of a river, not a spring. Wanting to obey Mary's request but not knowing how, Bernadette just started digging in the ground she was kneeling on. She began to eat the dirt, appalling those who had gathered for the apparition. Astonishingly, as she continued to dig, water began to pour out and, over the course of the day, it became a constant stream of fresh water that continues to this day.

This miraculous spring at Lourdes is now known for its healing powers when accompanied by faith and prayer. Millions of people visit the shrine every year in search of healing, both physical and spiritual. So far, there have been sixty-nine approved miracles with thousands more still in the process of seeking official approval.

Bernadette eventually became a nun with the Sisters of Charity, seeking to be hidden from the world. She did not want any recognition or credit and believed that Mary appeared to her because she was the lowest and the poorest of people. She simply sought to say yes to God through Mary, even when she didn't understand. We can see this both when she relayed her message to the priest about the identity of the woman and when she discovered the spring of healing waters. She died in 1879, at the age of thirty-five. Like St. Catherine Labouré, her body is incorrupt.

Mary, please give us the grace to say yes to God even when we don't understand.

Saint Bernadette Soubirous, pray for us.

---

[18] Ron Petak. "Who is Bernadette." Omaha World Herald (January 30, 2020): omaha.com/community/bellevue/who-is-st-bernadette/article_abb6f7c9-11b4-5ece-a6c6-faf575b59dbc.html.

Saint Maximilian Kolbe
(1894–1941)

Saint Maximilian Kolbe, who had a tremendous love for Mary, is known as the Apostle of Marian Consecration. Maximilian, whose birth name was Raymond, was born in Poland in 1894, the second of five boys (only three would survive to adulthood). He was a very rambunctious boy, causing his mother to one day exclaim, "Raymond, what will become of you!"[19] Raymond was twelve at the time and the statement really affected him. That night before bed, when he repeated the same question to the Blessed Virgin, she came to him and presented him with two crowns, one white and the other red. She asked him if he was willing to accept either of the crowns. The white crown meant that he would persevere in purity, while the red crown meant that he would become a martyr. He told her that he would accept both of them.

After that, Raymond developed a very deep love for Mary and later became a Franciscan priest with his older brother, Francis. As a Conventual Franciscan, he received the name Maximilian, meaning "greatest." He let the name constantly remind him that he wanted to be the "greatest" apostle of Marian Consecration that the world had ever seen. In 1917, Maximilian started the Militia Immaculata (MI), a movement that worked tirelessly for the conversion of sinners through consecration to Jesus through Mary.

For the next twenty years, Maximilian and the MI used every media outlet available to spread the message of Marian Consecration, and even founded monasteries in India, Poland, and Japan to try to reach more people. While Maximilian was a brilliant theologian who wrote extensively on different aspects of theology and taught in Polish seminaries, there was one thing that seemed to stump him. He could not understand why Mary

---

[19] Mary Felicitia Zdrojewski, CSSF, *To Weave a Garment: The Story of Maria Dabrowska Kolbe, Mother of Saint Maximilian Kolbe* (Enfield, CT: Felician Sisters, 1989), 148.

would identify herself as the Immaculate Conception to Bernadette at Lourdes. He knew, of course, that she was immaculately conceived, that is, conceived without the stain of Original Sin, because of the third Marian dogma proclaimed in 1854, but this seemed like she was trying to give a deeper understanding to her very identity.

Then, one day in the midst of World War II, he finally figured it out: Mary, being the spouse of the Holy Spirit, being "two in one flesh," also takes His Name. The Holy Spirit is the eternal and *uncreated* Immaculate Conception—the Love between God the Father and God the Son. Mary was so full of the Holy Spirit from the moment of her conception—conceived without Original Sin in preparation for the Incarnation—that she is the human reflection of the Holy Spirit, i.e., she is the incarnate and *created* Immaculate Conception.

This breakthrough has led to further insights about Mary and support what could one day be the fifth Marian dogma: Mary as Co-redemptrix, Mediatrix, Advocate. While Mary fully cooperates in her Son's redemptive mission, she is also an advocate for God's people and Mediatrix of all graces (God distributes His graces through her) since she is "one flesh" with the Holy Spirit, the advocate and giver of grace.

While this breakthrough itself was incredible, the timing made it even more so. Soon after Maximilian understood what Mary meant, he was arrested by the Nazis and taken to Auschwitz. The Nazis had been warning him to stop his public ministry, but he had refused. Maximilian ended up dying in Auschwitz on August 14, 1941, as a martyr of charity, offering to take the place of Franciszek Gajowniczek, who had been chosen at random to be starved to death. Gajowniczek, who had pleaded for his life because he had a wife and family, was present at Kolbe's canonization on October 10, 1982. The Militia Immaculate continues to work tirelessly for Marian Consecration. And the monastery in Nagasaki, Japan, that was founded by the martyr? It was untouched by the atomic bomb.

Mary, help us become who God created us to be.

Saint Maximilian Kolbe, pray for us.

Pope Venerable Pius XII
(1876–1958)

In 1950, almost one hundred years after the proclamation of the third Marian dogma of the Immaculate Conception, Pope Ven. Pius XII promulgated the fourth Marian dogma, the Assumption of Mary. This was an official proclamation of the Church's long-held belief that Mary was free from the "corruption of the grave," which is itself a consequence of Original Sin. The Assumption of Mary states that once her time on earth was done, she was taken up body and soul into the glory of Heaven.

Let's take a closer look at the pope who proclaimed this dogma. Pius XII was born Eugenio Maria Giuseppe Giovanni Pacelli to a very devout family in Rome. After being elected pope in 1939, he led the Church during the very challenging years of World War II, accomplishing many things in secret throughout his nineteen years as pope. Among other things, he recruited a group of priests to serve as spies during World War II, which ultimately led the Church to save over 850,000 Jews across Europe, including thousands of Jews in Rome that were hidden in either the Vatican or other Roman monasteries. He also spearheaded a secret archaeological dig to find the remains of St. Peter, the first pope, beneath the Basilica of St. Peter. In all this, he was very public about his devotion and love for Mary.

Pius XII had been consecrated as an archbishop on May 13, 1917, the day of the first apparition of Mary at Fatima, a connection that he believed to be very important. As pope, he wanted to fulfill her request to consecrate Russia to her Immaculate Heart, and, for this reason, in 1942, one year after the death of Maximilian Kolbe, in addition to the consecration of Russia, he consecrated the whole world to her Immaculate Heart and asked every Catholic family to consecrate themselves to her as well. In 1953, he became the first pope ever to declare a Marian year, and he installed several new Marian feast days, including the Assumption of Mary, the Queenship of Mary, and the Immaculate Heart of Mary.

Pope Pius XII was instrumental in furthering the understanding of Mary's role in the Church and for each of her children. But he was also very careful in pointing out that a strong Marian devotion leads to a stronger love for and better understanding of Jesus. In proclaiming any Marian dogma, there is simultaneously a truth about Jesus being revealed, since her role is always to bring us closer to Him.

Mary, lead us to a stronger love for and better understanding of Jesus.

Pope Venerable Pius XII, pray for us.

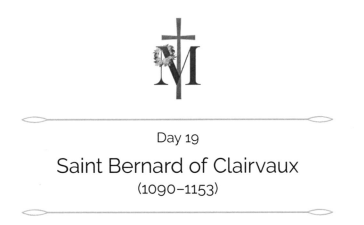

Day 19

Saint Bernard of Clairvaux
(1090–1153)

Pope Pius XII established the feast day of Mary Queen of Heaven in 1954. In reference to this important celebration in the Church, it is fitting to talk about St. Bernard of Clairvaux, who had such a strong love for Mary, especially under the title Queen of Heaven.

Bernard, who is one of thirty-six Doctors of the Church and is known as the Marian Doctor, was born in France in 1090, the third of seven children in a family with six boys and one girl. Growing up, Bernard was very well liked by everyone and had a charming personality, which made people naturally want to follow him. After the death of his mother at nineteen, Bernard prayed that Mary would show herself as his mother, and, one day when praying in the Church, he had a vision of her. Mary appeared holding the infant Jesus and gave Bernard the gift of wisdom. At that moment, he experienced the love of God in a very personal way and fully understood matters of the Faith. This set his heart on fire for love of God. Not long after, while praying in Church, he felt God was calling him to leave the world, join the monastery, and become a Cistercian monk. While telling the townspeople about his experience of God's love for him through the intercession of Mary, their hearts were set on fire too. When he set out for the monastery, thirty men from his town went with him. All but one of his brothers joined, and the last one joined them a few months later with their father. Talk about a good preacher!

Monasteries at the time were becoming extravagant, and the monks were becoming increasingly lazy towards their duties. When Bernard arrived at the monastery, he immediately began to live differently: fasting from both food and sleep, living in poverty, and caring for the poor. He preached the idea of a personal and intimate relationship with Jesus through Mary as intercessor, basing it off of his own conversion experience. Not surprisingly, the other men followed his lead and, pretty soon, the monastery was thriving.

It was said that Bernard was so rooted in Scripture that he could not talk without quoting it. He used his preaching skills for many things regarding the Faith, including being the "hype man" for the Christians in the Second Crusade, preaching to the soldiers before they set out to fight. But he is known primarily as the Marian Doctor because of his love for Mary and her intercession in bringing him to Jesus. Along with his preaching, he also wrote about her, including a beautiful meditation about the Annunciation, and a prayer to Mary as Star of the Sea. He also loved referring to Mary as the Queen of Heaven, a title rooted in Scripture. This fact was acknowledged one hundred and fifty years later when Dante Alighieri included St. Bernard in his epic poem *Paradiso* in *The Divine Comedy*. In the poem, St. Bernard prays, "And the Queen of heaven, for whom I burn completely with love, will give every grace, for I am her faithful Bernard."[20]

Mary's intercession transformed Bernard's life, and his life's goal was to show how her intercession always brings us to a deeply personal and intimate relationship with Jesus.

Mary, intercede for us that we may have a deeply personal and more intimate relationship with Jesus.

Saint Bernard of Clairvaux, pray for us.

---

[20] Dante Alighieri, *The Divine Comedy*, Paradiso, XXXI.

Saint Simon of Cyrene
(First Century)

As seen in the life of Simon of Cyrene, Mary's intercession can bring "good" out of "bad" and "better" out of "good." The Gospels recount how Jesus struggled to carry His Cross through the streets of Jerusalem. As the Cross became too heavy for Him, He collapsed (the Third Station of the Cross), prompting His mother to rush to His side (the Fourth Station). When Jesus was unable to carry the Cross any further, the Roman soldiers summoned a passer-by, Simon of Cyrene, to help Him carry His Cross the rest of the way to Calvary (the Fifth Station).

It seems appropriate that a man named Simon would help Jesus carry His Cross, especially considering that another Simon—Simon Peter—had promised Jesus just the night before, "Even if I must die with you, I will not deny you" (Mt 26:35). But after his threefold denial, Peter was not there, so Simon of Cyrene, a man who did not know Jesus, was summoned from the crowd instead. Also, I don't think it is a coincidence that Simon of Cyrene comes right after Mary. We can suppose that Mary, at this moment, was praying for her Son, and that her intercession brought some "good" out of the "bad" situation.

However, if we look a little deeper in the Gospel, we will see Mary's intercession at this moment actually brought "better" out of the "good." Not only did Simon of Cyrene help carry the Cross of Jesus, but, after encountering Jesus, his life was changed forever.

In the Gospel of Mark we read that "[the soldiers] compelled a passer-by, Simon of Cyrene, who was coming in from the country, the father of Alexander and Rufus, to carry his cross" (15:21). At first glance, mentioning the names of his sons seems insignificant. However, Mark was writing to the Gentile converts of Rome. Thus, these names of Alexander and Rufus must have been important, especially if they were now members of the Church in Rome! This is further reinforced in St. Paul's Letter to the Romans, when he says, "Greet Rufus, eminent in the Lord, also his mother and mine" (16:13). Sometime between the Resurrection of Jesus and St. Paul's Letter to the Romans, Simon's family had gone to Rome, where they were instrumental in helping to establish the Church. Through Mary's intercession, one man was led to encounter Jesus, which changed not only his life, but the life of his family, and the lives of countless others. Thus, out of the "bad" of Peter's denial, we have the "good" of Simon of Cyrene carrying the Cross and the "better" of Peter's renewed relationship with Jesus AND an entire family of new followers whose hearts have been set on fire with love for Jesus.

Mary, please bring "good" out of our "bad" and "better" out of our "good."

Saint Simon of Cyrene, pray for us.

Day 21

Saint Louis-Marie Grignion de Montfort

(1673-1716)

Saint Louis-Marie Grignion de Montfort could have easily been the saint we started this entire Marian Consecration with, considering how substantial he was—and continues to be—in promoting Marian Consecration in the Church. He is perhaps best known for his books on Marian Consecration, in particular *True Devotion to Mary* and *Total Consecration to Jesus Christ through Mary*. Many popes over the last one hundred and fifty years, including Pope Pius XII and Pope St. John Paul II, have urged the faithful to follow de Montfort's guidance and consecrate, or give, themselves "to Jesus through Mary."[21]

De Montfort was born in 1673, the second oldest of eighteen children in the small town of Montfort, France. He attended school at the local Jesuit college where his uncle was a priest. It was during this time that he developed a love for Mary and for Jesus present in the Blessed Sacrament. After attending seminary in Paris, Louis felt a deep desire to minister to the poor and requested to become a missionary and evangelize in the Americas. However, his request was denied, and he was sent instead to travel and preach in his home country.

As de Montfort preached, he noticed how poorly formed the people were, and he encountered some regions of France that were deep in heresy. In order to bring the people back to the truth, he began preaching about the effectiveness of Marian Consecration, the importance of devotion to the Eucharist, especially in Mass and Adoration, and the power of the daily Rosary. He worked exhaustively, preaching throughout all of France, until his death in 1716. Unfortunately, upon his death, his writings were essentially lost. In fact, he had said that the devil hated this work so much that he would hide it for over one hundred years—and that prophecy proved true. His writings weren't found until 1842, the same year that Marie-Alphonse

---

[21] See St. Louis de Montfort, *True Devotion to Mary*, Part II.

Ratisbonne received the Marian apparition in Rome. After verification that it was free of doctrinal error, *True Devotion to Mary* was published in 1853 and has since been a catalyst in the conversions of numerous people, many of whom have become great saints in the Church.

In *True Devotion to Mary*, de Montfort explains that Marian Consecration is the surest, easiest, shortest, and the most perfect means to becoming a saint.[22] He teaches us that Mary forms us into other Christs, or rather, in giving ourselves to her, she brings us closer to Him and He lives through us.

Mary, form us into other Christs.

Saint Louis-Marie Grignion de Montfort, pray for us.

---

[22] See St. Louis de Montfort, *True Devotion to Mary*, 55.

Day 22

Venerable Jan Tyranowski
(1901–1947)

Jan Tyranowski, who was born in 1901, in Krakow, Poland, was one of the many people affected by St. Louis de Montfort's *True Devotion to Mary* and *Total Consecration to Jesus Through Mary*. Jan was known as somewhat of a recluse and a little odd to those who encountered him. He never married or had children and lived with his mother most of his life. In fact, there seemed to be nothing very special about Jan, who lived his days working in his tailoring business and spending most nights at home.

However, during World War II in the early 1940s, Jan was called upon to help at the parish. At this point, the situation in Poland had become especially bad. In addition to targeting Jews, the Gestapo had started arresting priests, leaving the people without the spiritual guidance they so desperately needed. When this happened, people in the parish were asked to step in and help where they could, including Jan.

While Jan had been Catholic all his life, he had started to become more serious about his faith five years earlier, in 1935, when a priest, during his homily, said, "It is not difficult to become a saint."[23] That statement changed Jan's whole life, and he began to devote more and more time to prayer and spiritual reading, creating a deep interior life. Still, when asked to help out at the parish by mentoring a group of college men, he struggled with the idea because he felt he had very little to offer them. But, in the end, he reluctantly agreed, deciding to teach the group about what he knew and loved, especially St. Louis de Montfort's Marian Consecration. So he took in fifteen young adult men and called them the Living Rosary Group.

One of the members of this group was a young man named Karol Wojtyla. Karol had moved to Krakow from Wadowice, Poland, and, by the time these two men met, Karol had already lost his whole family. Jan became Karol's

---

[23] Andrew Swafford. "It's Not Difficult to Be a Saint." Chastity Project (January 23, 2018): chastity.com/2018/01/not-difficult-saint/.

mentor, friend, and spiritual director in their time together. It was at Jan's feet that Karol fell in love with Mary and became very convicted of the power of Marian Consecration. Jan introduced Karol to a deep spiritual life and walked with him as he sought to discover his life's vocation. It was through the guidance of Jan that Karol realized his vocation to the priesthood, and he was ordained to the priesthood just a few months before Jan died.

Karol later became the beloved—and now saint—Pope John Paul II, whose papal motto, *Totus Tuus*, came from St. Louis de Montfort's *True Devotion to Mary*, which was introduced to him by Jan Tyranowski, the mentor who proved to be instrumental in his early adulthood.[24]   Jan had no idea of the impact that his small yes would have on the Church for generations to come, but he gave his yes to what was being asked of him in that moment. He is a perfect example of giving what little we have to Mary and letting her bring it to her Son to bless and multiply it.

Pope John Paul II officially opened Jan Tyranowski's cause for canonization in 1997, and, in 2007, he was named venerable, the second step in the canonization process.

Mary, bring what little we have to your Son and ask Him to bless and multiply it.

Venerable Jan Tyranowski, pray for us.

---

[24] St. Louis de Montfort, *True Devotion to Mary*, 216

Day 23

Pope Saint John Paul II
(1920–2005)

Yesterday, we saw how Karol Wojtyla, the future Pope St. John Paul II, learned about Marian Consecration through his mentor, Jan Tyranowski. Karol Joseph Wojtyla was born in Wadowice, Poland, the youngest of three children. Unfortunately, his older sister died before Karol was born, and his mother died when he was just a boy. These deaths were followed by the deaths of his brother and then his father, leaving him with no immediate family by the time he was twenty-one years old. His father, a man in love with God, had a strong impact on Karol's faith life, especially in two ways. Shortly after his mother died, Karol's father brought him to a statue of Mary and told him, 'This is your mother now,"[25] placing his child under the care of Our Lady. As an adult, Karol recalled another way that his father's faith life deeply impacted his own. While growing up, Karol would wake up in the middle of the night and see his father kneeling in front of a crucifix in prayer. Through the example of his father, seeds of love for the Faith were planted in Karol—seeds that would grow into the great loves of his life.

John Paul Two, as he is commonly known, had arguably one of the greatest impacts on the Catholic Church and the world in modern times. He played a major role in the fall of Communism, he established Divine Mercy Sunday, and he canonized more saints than any other pope in history. However, it was his love for Mary that colored it all. When John Paul II was elected pope in 1979—the first non-Italian pope in over 500 years!—he chose *Totus Tuus* as his papal motto. These words, which come from St. Louis de Montfort's *True Devotion to Mary*, mean "Totally Yours" and are derived from the longer phrase *Totus tuus ego sum*, meaning "I am totally yours, and all that I have is yours."[26] This is a short Marian Consecration prayer in itself.

---

[25] Stephen Moss. "Your mother is dead. The Virgin Mary is your mother now." The Guardian (April 5, 2005): theguardian.com/world/2005/apr/05/catholicism.religion10.
[26] St. Louis de Montfort, *True Devotion to Mary*, 216.

One story in particular portrays the strength of the relationship between John Paul II and Mary. On Wednesday, May 13, 1981, on the sixty-fourth anniversary of the apparitions at Fatima, John Paul II was greeting the people gathered in St. Peter's Square for his Wednesday audience. As he traveled around the square in the popemobile, a trained assassin Mehmet Ali Ağca opened fire at close range. John Paul II was hit with four bullets, two of which lodged in his intestines. The pope should have been killed instantly, but Mary's hand was in the details of what happened next. Rushed to the hospital in the brand-new ambulance that he had blessed the day before—particularly blessing the first patient to ride in it—he arrived at the hospital in record time. Then, after surgery, the doctor said that as the bullet entered his stomach, it had changed course, narrowly avoiding any major arteries and saving his life. John Paul II reflected on this later and said, "One hand pulled the trigger, another guided the bullet."[27]   Seeing the significance of the date (the anniversary of the apparitions of Mary at Fatima), John Paul II knew it was Mary who had saved his life. To thank her, he flew to Fatima the next year and, repeating the actions of Pope Pius XII, consecrated the world again to the Immaculate Heart of Mary. Before he left Fatima, he placed the bullet that was supposed to have killed him in the crown of the Our Lady of Fatima statue, where it remains today.

John Paul II's relationship with Mary led him to a deeper love for Jesus, particularly in the Eucharist and in the people around him. He explained that becoming a son to Mary made him an even stronger disciple of Jesus. He would spend entire nights in his private adoration chapel, and it is said that he could sense the presence of the Blessed Sacrament, even if it was behind an unmarked door. His great love for those around him attracted people to him, especially the young. And, like Mary, John Paul II always led them to Jesus.

Mary, help us always lead others to Jesus.

Pope Saint John Paul II, pray for us.

---

[27] Fr. Gabriel Gillen. "One Hand Pulled the Trigger, Another Guided the Bullet." St. John Paul II Society (February 13, 2017): stjohnpaul.org/one-hand-pulled-the-trigger-another-guided-the-bullet/.

Day 24
The Fatima Children:
Servant of God Lucia
(1907–2005)
and Saints Francisco and Jacinta
(1908–1919) (1910–1920)

In 1917, Mary, who identified herself as the Lady of the Rosary—we now refer to her in these apparitions as Our Lady of Fatima—appeared in Fatima, Portugal to three shepherd children: Lucia, who was ten years old, and her cousins Francisco and Jacinta, who were eight years old and seven years old respectively. At the time, Fatima's situation reflected most of Europe—their young men were fighting in World War I, there was a rising tide of socialism and hostility towards the Church, and almost everyone was living in poverty and uncertainty. At the time Mary first appeared, the war in Europe had been raging for almost three years, and the Portuguese government was doing their best to exterminate Catholicism in Portugal.

In these apparitions, Mary begged the children to pray the Rosary for peace, pleading with the world to change their ways and turn back to God. On May 13, 1917, during her first apparition, Mary told the three children that she would return to the same spot on the thirteenth day of the month for the next six months. Unfortunately, throughout the next six months, the children would face persecution and suffering, especially from the town's atheist leaders. They consistently tried to pressure the children into saying that they were lying about the apparitions, and even had them arrested on August 13 so they were unable to go to the apparition—Mary ended up appearing to them on August 19 after their release from prison. But, as word spread about the apparitions, more and more people were beginning to show up. In one of her visits, Mary told the three children that the current war would end soon but if the world did not convert and change its ways, there would be a greater war in the future. World War I did end less than a year later, and her prophecy of another greater war was realized in World War II.

Throughout the apparitions, Mary also asked for the consecration of Russia to her Immaculate Heart to combat the spread of Communism. She always asked the children to pray the daily Rosary for peace in the world and the conversion of sinners, teaching them a prayer to say at the end of every decade of the Rosary for these intentions: "Oh my Jesus, forgive us our sins, save us from the fires of hell. Lead all souls to heaven, especially those in most need of thy mercy."[28]

In the July 13 apparition, Mary showed the children three secrets that had to do with the world and its future. These were to be written down and kept secret from the world until Mary said it was time to reveal them. While the first two secrets were revealed in 1941, the third and last secret was kept from the public until 2000. Before that, only the pope was allowed to read it. When it was finally released, it revealed a vision of a persecuted Church: a bishop dressed in white (the pope) being shot and killed along with other members of the Church. John Paul II believed that he was the pope mentioned in the third secret and understood that the day he was shot, May 13, 1981, connected him intimately to that prophetic vision. He came to realize that it was through the prayers of the faithful and the intercession of Mary that he was saved from death, showing how prayer can change the course of history.

The last apparition in Fatima happened on October 13, 1917. By that time, word had spread that Mary promised a miracle on this date. The day started with torrential rain but still 70,000 people showed up: believers, atheists, journalists, etc. When Mary appeared, the three children could see that she was accompanied by Jesus and Joseph, who blessed the gathered crowd. Suddenly, the rain stopped and the sun started dancing, appearing to plummet to the earth before shooting back up into the sky. After about ten minutes, the miracle ended and all 70,000 people were completely dry.

Only a year after the apparitions at Fatima ended, Francisco and Jacinta both died from the flu pandemic that devastated the world beginning in 1918. Both were canonized in 2017 on the 100th anniversary of the first apparition. Living to be ninety-seven years old, Lucia became a Carmelite nun and worked to spread the message of Fatima until her death in 2005. She was present when John Paul II made his pilgrimage of thanksgiving to Fatima in 1982.

Mary, intercede with us for peace in the world and a conversion of sinners.

Servant of God Lucia, and Saints Francisco and Jacinta, pray for us.

---

[28] Mary Thierfelder. "Five Prayers Taught at Fatima by Mary & the Angels." The Catholic Company/Magazine (May 10, 2017): catholiccompany.com/magazine/five-prayers-taught-at-fatima-by-mary-the-angels-6057

Day 25

Saint Padre Pio
(1887–1968)

Saint Padre Pio was born in 1887 in Pietrelcina, Italy, one of five surviving children. He was named Francesco, after St. Francis of Assisi, and he followed in the footsteps of some of the great Marian saints whom we have talked about before. Francesco and his family attended Mass together every day and prayed the Rosary as a family every night. He had a very strong Marian devotion his whole life and was one of those special souls who was able to see Jesus, Mary, and his guardian angel. From the young age of five, Francesco knew that he wanted to become a priest. He eventually followed in the footsteps of his patron, St. Francis of Assisi, and became a Franciscan Capuchin friar, receiving the name of Pio.

Pio lived only a few hours away from the Shrine of Our Lady of the Rosary in Pompeii, Italy. He was only a boy when it was restored and frequently visited it throughout his young adult years. His devotion to the Rosary throughout his life was so great that one day, when asked how many Rosaries he prayed daily, he replied, "Thirty-five"![29]   Astounded, the person asked him how he could he pray that much, to which Padre Pio replied, "How can you not?" Mary was his constant companion, and his love for her was reflected on the doorpost in his room where he wrote a quote from St. Bernard of Clairvaux, "Mary is the reason of all my hope."[30]

Six years after becoming a priest, Padre Pio was sent to San Giovanni Rotondo in Italy to the monastery of Our Lady of Grace, where he spent the remaining fifty-two years of his life. His schedule consisted of a 5 am daily Mass that lasted about three hours before dedicating the rest of his day to hearing confessions. Hundreds, if not thousands, of people left Padre Pio's confessional over the years with a newfound encounter of and love for

---

[29] Jeffrey S. J. Allan. "How Many Rosaries?!" Secret Harbour – Portus Secretioris (September 23, 2009): secret-harbor.blogspot.com/2009/09/how-many-rosaries.html.

[30] Brother Francis Mary F.I. "Our Lady in Padre Pio's Life." Pierced Hearts: piercedhearts.org/theology_heart/writings_on_saints/padre_pio_our_lady_brother_francis.htm.

Jesus. Word spread of radically changed lives—people who were more joyful, peaceful, loving, and patient—and soon others would travel—and sometimes wait for days—just for Padre Pio to hear their confessions. Seeing that Mary was always with him, there is no doubt that she, along with her Spouse, the Holy Spirit, was with him in the confessional as well. The Holy Spirit gives many gifts, including those that help us to make a good confession such as the gift of illumination to know our sins, the courage to confess them, true sorrow when asking for absolution, and the conviction to change. The Holy Spirit can transform a sinner's heart that was once filled with sin and fill it with His gifts—the first of which is always a deeper revealing of Jesus and His love.

With Mary and the Holy Spirit with him all day long, it's no wonder that Padre Pio had so many spiritual gifts, one of which was the ability to read souls so as to prompt people to confess sins they had forgotten or were hiding. He was able to bilocate in order to minister to different people in different places at the same time. These visits were sometimes accompanied by miraculous healings. He also had the gift of prophecy, and once, while meeting with Archbishop Karol Wojtyla of Krakow, who had traveled to San Giovanni Rotondo to meet with him, he prophesied to the archbishop that he would be pope one day. That prophecy proved true, and that man, Pope John Paul II, had the privilege of canonizing Padre Pio, declaring him a saint.

In Marian Consecration, it is suggested that we go to confession before our consecration day in order to empty ourselves of our sins. In this way, the Holy Spirit will be able to flood us with His gifts and graces, especially as we entrust our lives to his spouse, the Blessed Virgin Mary. Together, they will lead us to Jesus. Padre Pio's witness and the countless lives changed in his confessional are good reasons to follow through on that suggestion.

Mary, please come with me to the confessional and bring your Spouse, the Holy Spirit.

Saint Padre Pio, pray for us.

Day 26

Venerable Maria Teresa Quevedo
(1930–1950)

Maria Teresa Quevedo, affectionately known as Teresita, was born in Madrid, Spain, the youngest of three children to a very devout and loving family deeply rooted in their love for the Catholic Faith. When she was young, her parents took great care to teach her the Faith, and her father taught her to pray a morning offering, offering each day to Jesus through Mary. They talked about the saints and the martyrs of the Church, a topic very close to home in the early years of her life when the Spanish Civil War broke out and the government killed thousands of Catholics, including three of her uncles. But the family maintained their faith, and each night they would gather to pray the Rosary together as a family.

As a child, Teresita was stubborn and sensitive, but very sincere in her efforts to become a saint—a goal she wrote in her journal when she was ten years old. Showing her stubbornness and matter of fact manner, she wrote, "I have decided to become a saint."[31] She decided to take Mary as her companion to ensure her success. Teresita loved her Faith and loved to share it with others, and she had a special love for the Rosary. In fact, she taught her cook and her nurse how to pray the Rosary, and, after making the promise to pray the Rosary every day after school in front of Jesus in the Blessed Sacrament, she taught many of her friends how to pray the Rosary as well. While in school she joined a Marian Consecration group inspired by the writings of St. Louis de Montfort. She was encouraged to choose a motto when she became a member, and she wrote a simple but beautiful prayer that she would repeat for the rest of her life: "Mother, let all who look at me see You."[32]

Teresita was well loved by her classmates and was very outgoing and fun. She also loved fashion, and, when her friends couldn't see the connection

---

[31] Cromly, Nathan, *Totus Tuus: A Contemplative Approach to Total Consecration to Jesus through Mary* (United States: Marian Faith Network, 2013), 194.

[32] Cromly, *Totus Tuus: A Contemplative Approach to Total Consecration to Jesus through Mary*, 196.

between that and her love for Jesus, she would say that Jesus loves beautiful things too. However, she knew it was her inner beauty—her desire for holiness—that Jesus loved more, and she vowed to leave her love of fashion at the convent doorstep the day she became a Carmelite nun.

As she grew up, and even after she entered the Carmelites at the young age of seventeen, she continued to struggle with her faults, having been accused of being too dramatic, too spontaneous, and too impatient, even in her work. But she was determined to continue to give her soul totally to Mary, knowing that Mary would give it to Jesus, and Jesus, who never refuses His mother, would then make it "perfect, as our Heavenly Father is perfect" (Mt 5: 38). She trusted totally that Mary's intercession would fill the gap between who she was and who God created her to be, so she could become a saint.

Her life would prove to be a short one. In the winter of 1949, when Teresita became sick, she asked those around her to pray her short prayer to Mary if ever a time came when she couldn't talk. In April 1950, one week before her twentieth birthday, Teresita died. Her cause for canonization was opened four years later, and she is currently a venerable in the Catholic Church, the second step in the canonization process.

"Mother, let all who look at me see You."

Venerable Maria Teresa Quevedo, pray for us.

Day 27

Saint Anthony of Padua
(1195–1231)

Saint Anthony of Padua was born Fernando Bulhões in Lisbon, Portugal in 1195 into a wealthy family, and, as a young man, he joined the local Augustinian Order. After seeing the bodies of five Franciscan friars who had been martyred by Muslims while trying to evangelize in Morocco, his heart was set on fire, and he longed to evangelize as well. Not having that option in the Augustinian Order, he asked to be released from the Augustinians and set off to find the man who founded the Franciscans, St. Francis of Assisi.

From the time they met, Anthony and Francis were kindred spirits—they were both on fire with love for Jesus through their strong personal devotion to Mary. The two men inspired this strong devotion in their brother friars and created the foundation for what is now a pillar of the Franciscan Order, preaching not only Jesus, but devotion to Mary as the way to Him. Throughout his life, St. Anthony strove to be another Mary in the world, a creature who constantly contemplated God and His heavenly things while also pointing others to Him. It is only fitting, then, that St. Anthony is most often pictured holding the Child Jesus in his arms, an image inspired by the story told by a fellow friar who saw light coming from Anthony's room late one night, and, after peaking in, saw Anthony holding and talking to the Infant Jesus.

Anthony's deep insights on Mary led him to understand that she was immaculately conceived, assumed into Heaven, and now serves as Queen of Heaven—truths that would not be infallibly declared by the Church for another six centuries. It was these insights that led him to know deeper truths about Jesus and His Church—insights that he not only shared with his fellow friars, but would preach about publicly. His public preaching and teaching of his fellow Franciscans made him an extremely effective evangelist, earning him the title of Doctor of the Church, and he is known as the Evangelical Doctor.

Anthony died in Padua, Italy, in 1231, just five years after St. Francis, and he was declared a saint within the year. We remember him mostly as the saint who helps us find our lost things, but his impact, along with that of St. Francis, in instilling a Marian devotion in the Franciscan Order has continued on through the centuries and continues to bear fruit in our world today.

Mary, help me to be another you in the world.

Saint Anthony of Padua, pray for us.

Saint Ignatius of Loyola
(1491–1556)

Saint Ignatius of Loyola was born in the Basque country of Spain and was the youngest of thirteen children. His older brother married the maid of Queen Isabella, the Queen of Spain, who financed the exploration of Christopher Columbus when Ignatius was only one year old. The queen gifted the couple with a beautiful painting of the Annunciation, and, in order to have a proper place to put it, the couple built a chapel at the Loyola castle. So Ignatius grew up with a chapel at home that housed this beautiful image of Mary, planting a seed for his devotion later in life.

As he grew older, Ignatius dreamed of becoming a knight. He was vain in his image and strove to make a name for himself amongst the nobility of Spain. All of this changed when Ignatius was injured during a battle in which his leg was shattered by a cannonball. Upon returning home, his sister-in-law nursed him back to health and provided him with spiritual readings that awakened in him a desire for the spiritual life. However, Ignatius continued to struggle with his old vices until one day when Mary came to him with the baby Jesus. This encounter changed his life and gave him the grace to desire to live a life for Jesus, being led by Mary. In order to show his seriousness in changing his life, Ignatius made a pilgrimage to a hermitage on top of a mountain near Barcelona and placed his sword at the feet of Our Lady of Montserrat, giving himself to her and begging her to form him into another Jesus.

Ignatius, taking Mary as his guide, began down this path of holiness at the age of thirty. He enrolled in the University of Paris to receive a formal education, and it was there that he met his two roommates, Francis Xavier and Peter Faber, both of whom were in their early twenties. Ignatius began teaching these two men about all he had experienced in his recent conversion, and his powerful witness awakened in them a desire to join him on his quest for Heaven. Together, the three of them, along with four other classmates, founded the Society of Jesus, popularly known as the

Jesuits. These men asked Mary to be their main intercessor and, together, at the statue of Mary at St. Paul Outside the Walls in Rome, they made their official vows as Jesuits.

Throughout his life, Ignatius constantly begged Mary to help him do God's will, always turning to her in his discernment of what he thought God was asking of him. Born out of this were his writings known as the Spiritual Exercises in which he strove to help others discern God's will for them while drawing off of his own experiences of what worked and what didn't work in the spiritual life. Seeing the great power of Mary's intercession in his own life, Ignatius mentions her frequently throughout the Exercises, encouraging her intercession in contemplating God's will for our lives. Ignatius teaches us that in order to stay faithful to our vocations and missions in life, which should always lead us closer to Jesus and help us lead others to Him, we must stay close to Mary.

Ignatius, along with his two roommates, would be canonized as saints. Ignatius is known as the founder of the Jesuits and patron of spiritual retreats, Francis Xavier is remembered as one of the greatest evangelizers of all time who baptized over 700,000 people, and Peter Faber was the first Jesuit priest who taught the Spiritual Exercises to the men who joined the Jesuit Order. By following God's will under the guidance and protection of Mary, Ignatius was able to awaken God's will in those around him too.

Mary, help us as we discern God's will for our lives.

Saint Ignatius of Loyola, pray for us.

Day 29

Saint Bridget of Sweden
(1303–1373)

Saint Bridget of Sweden was born in 1303 to a powerful knight and his wife, a distant relative of the king. Bridget was married at age thirteen to a holy and devout man, and together they had eight children. One of their daughters, Catherine of Sweden, is also a saint. After twenty years of marriage, and shortly after they returned from a pilgrimage to Santiago de Compostela, a famous and ancient pilgrimage site in northwestern Spain that is still popular today, her husband died. After his death, Bridget poured her life even more into prayer, serving the poor, raising her children, and working towards establishing a new religious order of nuns and priests.

From the time Bridget was a little girl, she was visited by Jesus and Mary, who showed her visions of the Nativity and the Crucifixion, along with visions of Purgatory. Her descriptions of these visions have largely influenced the Christian art of these scenes. Aside from these visions, Bridget also received two important devotions to Mary. The first, the Brigittine Rosary, which has six decades instead of five, with the sixth decade dedicated to events in the life of Mary. The Apostles' Creed is prayed after each decade instead of the Glory Be, and the sixty-three Hail Mary's are prayed in honor of the sixty-three years that Mary is said to have lived.

But Mary also gave St. Bridget another very important devotion— the Seven Sorrows of Mary. Mary explained that she longed for souls to keep her company, asking for an Our Father and Seven Hail Mary's to be prayed while reflecting on each of the Seven major sorrows of her life.

The Seven Sorrows of Mary
(Also known as the Seven Dolors of Mary)
1. The Prophecy of Simeon (Lk 2:34–35)
2. The Flight into Egypt (Mt 2:13–21)
3. The Loss of Jesus for Three Days (Lk 2:41–50)
4. The Carrying of the Cross (Lk 23:27–30)
5. The Crucifixion of Jesus (Jn 19:18–30)
6. Jesus is Taken Down from the Cross (Jn 19:38–40)
7. Jesus is Laid in the Tomb (Jn 19:39–42)

Mary revealed to Bridget that people who practiced devotion to the Seven Sorrows would receive great graces, including peace in their families, consolation in their pains, Mary's accompaniment in their work, and her visible presence to them at their death, bringing them right to Heaven. Jesus later appeared to Bridget and confirmed these promises.

In the years since Mary gave St. Bridget this devotion, Mary has appeared as Our Lady of Sorrows in several apparitions, including at Fatima and Kibeho. The Church now dedicates the month of September to Our Lady of Sorrows, and her feast day is September 15, the day after the Exaltation of the Holy Cross, commemorating the day that St. Helen discovered the Cross that Jesus was crucified on.

Mary, give us the grace of devotion to your Seven Sorrows.

Saint Bridget of Sweden, pray for us.

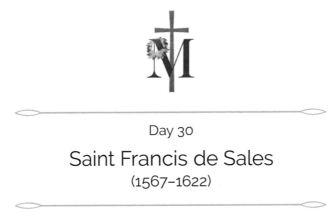

Day 30

Saint Francis de Sales
(1567–1622)

Saint Francis de Sales was born in the year 1567 to a wealthy family who lived in a castle near Geneva, Switzerland. He lived in the midst of the Protestant Reformation and died just six years before St. Louis de Montfort was born.

During his young adulthood, there was a debate going on between Catholics and Calvinists (Protestants) over predestination, the idea that certain souls were predestined for Heaven and certain souls predestined for Hell. Calvinists believed that no matter what people did on earth, they couldn't change their destiny. Suffering terribly with scruples—thinking everything he did was a sin—Francis became convinced that he was not a soul predestined for Heaven. This idea led him to almost complete despair. However, he loved God so much that he finally resolved that, even if he was not destined for Heaven, he would at least love God as much as he could during his earthly life. This thought of being predestined for Hell tortured him so much that one day he could not take it anymore. He ran to a statue of Mary and fell at her feet. He fervently prayed the *Memorare* prayer, begging her help and asking to know the truth in what he had come to believe. Immediately upon finishing his prayer, his mind was cleared, and he realized that what he believed about his destiny was not true and did not come from God. His burden was lifted, and he was free. He gained a renewed sense of love and vigor to serve Jesus. Seeing with clarity the tenderness of Mary's intercession and the power of the *Memorare*, Francis vowed to pray it every day of his life. He later attested that Mary had never left him "unaided," as promised in the prayer.

Francis went on to become a priest and later a bishop, gaining for himself a reputation as a smart and gentle man. He never forgot what it was like to suffer so badly but also to experience the tenderness of the Mother towards her son. Francis was renowned as a spiritual director and strove to treat others with patience and gentleness in their own interior struggles. His devotion to Mary was so great that, together with St. Jane Frances de

Chantal, he founded the religious order of the Visitation of Holy Mary, an order of women that live out the humility and gentleness of Mary, especially as shown in the Visitation with her cousin Elizabeth.

Throughout his life, Francis also devoted his Communion every Saturday to Mary and offered her some sort of hidden sacrifice. While the tradition of offering your Communion in honor of a specific devotion each day is not new, the Saturday devotion became more widely known when Mary requested the Five First Saturdays Devotion in Fatima almost three hundred years later. At Fatima, she asked that for five consecutive first Saturdays we go to Confession, receive Holy Communion, pray five decades of the Rosary, and keep her company for fifteen minutes while meditating on the mysteries of the Rosary. For those who will do this, she promised to assist them at the hour of death with the grace necessary for salvation.

Francis died due to a stroke in the year 1622 and was declared a Doctor of the Church. He is also known as the "Gentleman Saint" because of the humility, gentleness, and patience that he extended to all whom he met.

Mary, grant us the grace to be humble, gentle, and patient toward all those we meet.

Saint Francis de Sales, pray for us.

Day 31

Saint Alphonsus Liguori
(1696–1787)

Saint Alphonsus Liguori was born in 1696 near Naples, Italy, and was the oldest of seven children. His parents were very devout Catholics, and even gave him the name Mary as one of his middle names, thus foreshadowing his future devotion to his Queen and Mother. Growing up, Alphonsus was a brilliant student and graduated as a lawyer at the age of sixteen, quickly building a reputation as one of the best lawyers in the area. However, after about ten years of practicing law, Alphonsus decided to leave the public world and become a priest.

Alphonsus lived at the time of a devastating heresy in the Church called Jansenism, which was characterized by unforgiveness and extreme guilt that scared people away from receiving Holy Communion. Alphonsus took on this heresy with great zeal, preaching gentleness and the importance of mercy in the Sacrament of Confession, saying, "The penitents should be treated as souls to be saved rather than as criminals to be punished."[33] His battle for souls led him to write some incredible works on the power of devotion to Jesus in the Blessed Sacrament and Mary as Our Sorrowful Mother and Queen. Alphonsus also started the Congregation of the Most Holy Redeemer (the Redemptorists), an order of priests founded to fight the Jansenist heresy.

Alphonsus's love for Mary was evident in his life and in his work. He wrote a six hundred page collection of five books on the importance of Mary and her powerful intercession, which stemmed from his own experience and from the writings of other Doctors of the Church. Mary seemed to reward St. Alphonsus for this when, a little less than a century after he died, the famous icon of Our Lady of Perpetual Help miraculously found its permanent home in the Redemptorist Church of St. Alphonsus

---

[33] Ana St. Paul. "Saint of the Day – 1 August – St Alphonsus Maria de Liguori C.Ss.R. – Doctor of the Church." AnaStPaul (August 1, 2017): anastpaul.com/2017/08/01/saint-of-the-day-1-august-st-alphonsus-maria-de-liguori-c-ss-r-doctor-of-the-church/.

in Rome, Italy. It was only natural that Mary, under this title, would choose to be placed under the care of the Redemptorists, whose founder loved her so much.

This famous icon of Mary, as Queen and Sorrowful Mother, depicts her holding the frightened Child Jesus. The image shows us that, as the Mystical Body of Christ, we also have this same Mother whom we can run to when we need her. We are reminded of this in the *Memorare* prayer:

> Remember, O most gracious Virgin Mary,
> that never was it known that **anyone who**
> **fled to your protection,**
> implored your help, or sought your intercession was left unaided.
> **Inspired by this confidence, I fly unto you,**
> **O Virgin of virgins, my mother;**
> to you do I come, before you I stand, sinful and sorrowful.
> O Mother of the Word Incarnate, despise not my petitions,
> but in your mercy hear and answer me.
> Amen.

Mary, help us to run to you in our times of need.

Saint Alphonsus Liguori, pray for us.

Saint John Vianney
(1786–1859)

Saint John-Baptiste-Marie Vianney was born in 1786, near Lyon, France, just three years before the outbreak of the French Revolution, a time when the Catholic Church was heavily persecuted and priests were executed by the hundreds. Growing up, John's family remained faithful to their Catholicism, attending secret Masses in the middle of the night and hiding priests to save them from death. John saw these brave priests as heroes and decided that he too wanted to become a priest, putting his vocation under the care and protection of Mary.

From a very young age, John had a great love for Mary. As a boy, he had to drop out of school to help his family work in the fields, but, since he was still so young, he had a hard time keeping up with the pace of his older brother. After overhearing his brother complain about this to their mother, John had an idea. In order to keep up, he brought his beloved statue of Mary into the fields with him. John would kiss the statue of Mary and then throw it along the path he was working, motivating him to work as fast and as hard as he could in order to reach it. Then, once he reached it, he would pick up the statue, kiss it and throw it again. This process helped him to keep up with his brother in the fields.

As an adult, John was almost unable to become a priest due to his poor education. In fact, he was going to be dismissed from the seminary until his mentor, Fr. Bailey, decided to speak to the bishop about John personally. At the end of their discussion, the bishop decided to ordain John, not based on his test scores, but because Fr. Bailey answered an emphatic yes to the following three questions regarding John: Is he a pious man? Is he consecrated to Our Lady? Does he pray the Rosary?

After his ordination, the bishop assigned him to be the curé (village priest) of Ars, France, a small town that had not had a priest in over thirty years. He arrived to find the people with little or no devotion and overall a general ignorance of their Catholic Faith. John immediately consecrated his parish to Mary and then proceeded to go door to door to invite every parishioner back to the sacraments. For the first several months, his pews were empty, so he would preach with the doors to the Church wide open so all could hear his message. He invested in the lives of his parishioners with simple and direct words that ended up moving their hearts. John preached the power of Confession, along with devotion to the Eucharist and the power of Mary's intercession. More people began attending Sunday Mass and then came to him for Confession during the week. John always had Mary with him in the confessional and imitated her mercy when receiving sinners. He often said that the greater the sinner, the more they should be treated with tenderness and compassion.

John's reputation as a confessor spread to neighboring towns and soon he was spending up to seventeen hours a day in the confessional! However, the devil did not like that John was taking these people from him and bringing them back to their Catholic Faith. Almost every night, the devil would do things to try and scare John, and one night he even set his bed on fire. But his attempt to keep John from bringing people to Jesus was unsuccessful. The devil once admitted that this was because John was consecrated to Mary, and, when someone was under her protection, the devil was powerless.

Over the course of his time in Ars, John successfully brought every member of the town back into the Catholic Church and consecrated them to Mary. Now commonly known as the Curé of Ars, St. John Vianney is the patron saint of parish priests, and the cause for canonization of his mentor, Fr. Bailey, has been officially opened in the Church.

Mary, bring us under your protection.

Saint John Vianney, pray for us.

Servant of God Chiara Corbella Petrillo

(1984–2012)

Chiara Corbella was born on January 9, 1984, in Rome, Italy. She was the younger of two daughters in a devout Catholic family whose faith and Marian devotion were greatly influenced by the pope at the time, Pope St. John Paul II.

It was no surprise, then, that Mary would play a large role in Chiara's life, especially in her vocation as wife and mother. When she was just nineteen years old, Chiara met her future husband, Enrico Petrillo, on a Marian pilgrimage to Medjugorje. After six years of on-again, off-again dating, the couple became engaged while on a walking pilgrimage to St. Mary of the Angels Basilica in Assisi, Italy. This basilica became the place where they would frequently place their cares into the hands of Mary, consecrating themselves and all that they brought to her. It was here that they consecrated their engagement, their marriage, and all three of their children to Jesus through Mary.

Throughout their marriage, Chiara and Enrico turned to Mary in everything. Together, they began every day with their prayer of consecration, which ended with *Totus Tuus*, meaning totally yours, in which one entrusts everything to Jesus through Mary. This was both St. Louis de Montfort's prayer and Pope St. John Paul II's papal motto. Not long after they were married, Chiara and Enrico found out that she was pregnant. They were elated until their twentieth week appointment, when they were told their baby girl would not survive outside the womb. Chiara immediately thought of Mary. She, too, had a child she would watch die, but still said yes to God's will without fully understanding it. Chiara knew that God was also asking her to trust Him, to stay in the present moment, and to take the next small possible step. This grace of seeing Mary as her model gave Chiara joy in the midst of her great suffering. When their daughter was born, they named her Maria Grazia Letizia, meaning Mary of favor and joy.

When their second child, David Giovanni, also died shortly after birth, Chiara and Enrico again turned to Mary. They asked for her intercession for another baby, and soon Chiara became pregnant with a healthy baby boy. However, during her pregnancy, Chiara was diagnosed with carcinoma, a deadly form of cancer. Even though she refused treatment while pregnant in order to protect her baby, Chiara and Enrico began to rely even more heavily on the intercession of Mary. They had always prayed the Rosary together at night, but now they began to invite some family and friends to join them. Chiara's joy and peace when facing her imminent death touched everyone who came into contact with her.

In April of 2012, with all medical treatments exhausted, Chiara and Enrico decided to return to Medjugorje not only to ask for healing but also to ask for the grace to continue to take the next small possible step that God was asking of them. Even though Chiara did not receive the physical healing they asked for, they did receive the grace they needed to continue on their path with joy and trust. Enrico later reflected that it was Mary who showed them the way and told them, as she tells us, "Do whatever He tells you" (Jn 2:5). Chiara died on June 13, 2012, and her funeral was celebrated on the feast day of the Immaculate Heart of Mary.

Chiara's cause for sainthood was opened in September 2017, almost immediately after the required five-year wait period was over. She is currently a servant of God, the first step in the canonization process.

Mary, help us to take the next small possible step.

Servant of God Chiara Corbella Petrillo, pray for us.

Day 34
Consecration Day

Prayer of Consecration to Jesus through Mary

Oh Jesus, through the Immaculate Heart of Mary,

I consecrate myself to you totally and completely.

Mary, I give you all of my prayers, works, joy, and sufferings.

Please accept and perfect them by filling the gaps,

and then offer them to Jesus on my behalf.

Mary, bring me deeper into the Sacred Heart of Jesus.

Lend me your heart that I may love Him perfectly with it.

Please obtain for me all of the graces He has in store for me

and help me to experience His personal love for me in a new way.

If ever I am tempted to turn away from Jesus,

I ask that you remind me of this consecration

and help me to feel your motherly protection.

Grant me the grace to become who God has created me to be

and to follow Him even when I don't understand.

When others look at me, help them to see you,

and help me to lead others to Jesus as you do.

Mary, be with me as I continuously strive to do His will

by taking the next small possible step.

Lead me to His heavenly Kingdom. *Totus Tuus*.

Amen.

Litany of Petitions to Mary

Mary, please fill the gap.

Mary, take care of the details.

Mary, give us the grace to be faithful to the Rosary.

Mary, give us confidence in the promises of the Rosary.

Mary, send St. Michael and the heavenly army to defend us in battle.

Mary, please ask Jesus for the grace of repentance for us, for we know that He can refuse you nothing.

Mary, help us to develop a "heart relationship" with you and your Son.

Mary, lead us to the Truth.

Mary, our mother, please lend us your heart so that we may love Jesus perfectly and remain close to Him always.

Mary, help our families turn to you as our intercessor.

Mary, when our time comes, take us into your arms and bring us to Heaven.

Mary, help us to do whatever He tells us (see Jn 2: 5).

Mary, help us to say yes to what God is calling us to, even if it hasn't yet been done.

Mary, please obtain for us all of God's graces.

Mary, never leave us unaided.

Mary, please give us the grace to say yes to God even when we don't understand.

Mary, help us become who God created us to be.

Mary, lead us to a stronger love for and better understanding of Jesus.

Mary, intercede for us that we may have a deeply personal and more intimate relationship with Jesus.

Mary, please bring "good" out of our "bad" and "better" out of our "good."

Mary, form us into other Christs.

Mary, bring what little we have to your Son and ask Him to bless and multiply it.

Mary, help us always lead others to Jesus.

Mary, intercede for us for peace in the world and a conversion of sinners.

Mary, please come with me to the confessional and bring your Spouse, the Holy Spirit.

Mother, grant that everyone who looks at me may see you.

Mary, help me to be another you in the world.

Mary, help us as we discern God's will for our lives.

Mary, give us the grace of devotion to your Seven Sorrows.

Mary, grant us the grace to be humble, gentle, and patient toward all those we meet.

Mary, help us to run to you in our times of need.

Mary, bring us under your protection.

Mary, help us to take the next small possible step.

Amen.

Pittcraft Printing
Pittsburg, KS
www.pittcraft.com